I0081764

UNPRESIDENTED

The Trump Presidency in 1000 Tweets

Compiled by Jasper Robinett

Unpresidented: The Trump Presidency in 1000 Tweets © Jasper Robinett 2021

ISBN: 978-0-6488236-8-1 (paperback)

This publication is a collection of statements by the @Realdonaldtrump Twitter account from his time as President of the United States of America. In no way have the content of these tweets been edited or altered.

All rights reserved. No part of this publication may be reproduced, stored in a retrieval system, or transmitted in any form or by any means electronic, mechanical, photocopying, recording, or otherwise, without the prior written permission of the author.

Published in Australia by Jasper Robinett

A catalogue record for this
book is available from the
National Library of Australia

NATIONAL
LIBRARY
OF AUSTRALIA

CONTENTS

FOREWORD

A presidency is many things to many people. It charts the course of a nation, steers the dictates of power and navigates the twists and turns of the years. A presidency is as complex as it is important.

How, then, do we map a presidency?

When that president is Donald J Trump, the answer is easy. The president who has become synonymous with twitter, ought to be remembered for their tweets.

This is the Trump Presidency in 1000 of his most memorable, controversial, and informative tweets.

PREFACE

The following tweets have been compiled as direct quotes from Donald J. Trump's personal twitter account, @realDonaldTrump. No spelling, grammar or formatting changes have been made.

For example:

Nov 8, 2016

TODAY WE MAKE AMERICA
GREAT AGAIN!

Nov 9, 2016

Such a beautiful and important evening!
The forgotten man and woman will never be
forgotten again. We will all come together
as never before

2017

Jan 19, 2017

"It wasn't Donald Trump that
divided this country, this country has been
divided for a long time!"
Stated today by Reverend Franklin Graham.

Jan 20, 2017

the American people. I have no doubt that we
will, together, MAKE AMERICA
GREAT AGAIN!

Jan 21, 2017

A fantastic day and evening in
Washington D.C. Thank you to @FoxNews
and so many other news outlets for the
GREAT reviews of the speech!

Jan 21, 2017

January 20th 2017, will be remembered
as the day the people became the rulers of
this nation again.

Jan 22, 2017

Had a great meeting at
CIA Headquarters yesterday, packed house,
paid great respect to Wall, long standing
ovations, amazing people. WIN!

Jan 22, 2017

Watched protests yesterday but was under
the impression that we just had an election!
Why didn't these people vote?
Celebs hurt cause badly.

Jan 23, 2017

Peaceful protests are a hallmark of our
democracy. Even if I don't always agree,
I recognize the rights of people to
express their views.

Jan 25, 2017

If Chicago doesn't fix the horrible
"carnage" going on, 228 shootings in
2017 with 42 killings (up 24% from 2016),
1 will send in the Feds!

Jan 25, 2017

Big day planned on NATIONAL SECURITY
tomorrow. Among many other things,
we will build the wall!

Jan 28, 2017

Mexico has taken advantage of the U.S.
for long enough. Massive trade deficits &
little help on the very weak border
must change, NOW!

Jan 29, 2017

The failing @nytimes has been wrong
about me from the very beginning.
Said I would lose the primaries, then the
general election. FAKE NEWS!

Jan 30, 2017

...Senators should focus their energies
on ISIS, illegal immigration and
border security instead of always looking
to start World War III.

Jan 30, 2017

There is nothing nice about searching for
terrorists before they can enter our country.
This was a big part of my campaign.
Study the world!

Jan 31, 2017

If the ban were announced with a one week notice, the "bad" would rush into our country during that week. A lot of bad "dudes" out there!

Feb 1, 2017

Everybody is arguing whether or not it is
a BAN. Call it what you want, it is about
keeping bad people (with bad intentions)
out of country!

Feb 1, 2017

Hope you like my nomination of
Judge Neil Gorsuch for the
United States Supreme Court. He is a good
and brilliant man, respected by all.

Feb 2, 2017

Congratulations to Rex Tillerson
on being sworn in as our new
Secretary of State. He will be a star!

Feb 2, 2017

Do you believe it? The Obama
Administration agreed to take thousands of
illegal immigrants from Australia.
Why? I will study this dumb deal!

Feb 3, 2017

Thank you to Prime Minister of
Australia for telling the truth about
our very civil conversation that FAKE NEWS
media lied about. Very nice!

Feb 3, 2017

Yes, Arnold Schwarzenegger did a
really bad job as Governor of California
and even worse on the Apprentice...
but at least he tried hard!

Feb 5, 2017

The judge opens up our country to
potential terrorists and others that
do not have our best interests at heart.
Bad people are very happy!

Feb 6, 2017

Just cannot believe a judge would put our
country in such peril. If something
happens blame him and court system.
People pouring in. Bad!

Feb 7, 2017

I don't know Putin, have no deals in Russia,
and the haters are going crazy - yet
Obama can make a deal with Iran,
#1 in terror, no problem!

Feb 8, 2017

It is a disgrace that my full Cabinet is still
not in place, the longest such delay in the
history of our country.
Obstruction by Democrats!

Feb 12, 2017

Melania and I are hosting
Japanese Prime Minister Shinzo Abe and
Mrs. Abe at Mar-a-Lago in Palm Beach, Fla.
They are a wonderful couple!

Feb 15, 2017

This Russian connection non-sense is merely
an attempt to cover-up the many mistakes
made in Hillary Clinton's losing campaign.

Feb 17, 2017

Thank you for all of the nice statements
on the Press Conference yesterday.
Rush Limbaugh said one of greatest ever.
Fake media not happy!

Feb 19, 2017

Don't believe the main stream (fake news)
media.The White House is running
VERY WELL. I inherited a MESS and am
in the process of fixing it.

Feb 21, 2017

HAPPY PRESIDENTS DAY - MAKE
AMERICA GREAT AGAIN!

Feb 22, 2017

The so-called angry crowds in home
districts of some Republicans are actually,
in numerous cases, planned out
by liberal activists. Sad!

Feb 27, 2017

Russia talk is FAKE NEWS put out
by the Dems, and played up by the media,
in order to mask the big election defeat
and the illegal leaks!

Mar 2, 2017

THANK YOU!

Mar 4, 2017

Terrible! Just found out that Obama had my
"wires tapped" in Trump Tower just
before the victory. Nothing found.
This is McCarthyism!

Mar 5, 2017

Arnold Schwarzenegger isn't voluntarily
leaving the Apprentice, he was fired
by his bad (pathetic) ratings, not by me.
Sad end to great show

Mar 8, 2017

I have tremendous respect for women
and the many roles they serve that are
vital to the fabric of our society
and our economy.

Mar 8, 2017

Don't let the FAKE NEWS tell you that
there is big infighting in the Trump Admin.
We are getting along great, and getting
major things done!

Mar 13, 2017

It is amazing how rude much of the
media is to my very hard working
representatives. Be nice, you will do
much better!

Mar 14, 2017

ObamaCare is imploding. It is a disaster
and 2017 will be the worst year yet, by far!
Republicans will come together
and save the day.

Mar 15, 2017

Will be going to Detroit, Michigan (love),
today for a big meeting on bringing
back car production to State &
U.S. Already happening!

Mar 15, 2017

Can you imagine what the outcry would be if
@SnoopDogg, failing career and all,
had aimed and fired the gun at
President Obama? Jail time!

Mar 18, 2017

North Korea is behaving very badly.
They have been "playing" the
United States for years.
China has done little to help!

Mar 19, 2017

Despite what you have heard from the
FAKE NEWS, I had a GREAT meeting with
German Chancellor Angela Merkel.
Nevertheless, Germany owes…..

…vast sums of money to NATO & the
United States must be paid more for the
powerful, and very expensive,
defense it provides to Germany

Mar 28, 2017

Why isn't the House Intelligence
Committee looking into the
Bill & Hillary deal that allowed big
Uranium to go to Russia, Russian speech....

...money to Bill, the Hillary Russian
"reset," praise of Russia by Hillary,
or Podesta Russian Company. Trump Russia
story is a hoax. #MAGA!

Apr 1, 2017

When will Sleepy Eyes Chuck Todd and @
NBCNews start talking about the
Obama SURVEILLANCE SCANDAL
and stop with the Fake Trump/Russia story?

Apr 3, 2017

Did Hillary Clinton ever apologize
for receiving the answers to the debate?
Just asking!

Apr 9, 2017

It was a great honor to have
President Xi Jinping and Madame Peng Liyuan
of China as our guests in the
United States. Tremendous...

...goodwill and friendship was formed,
but only time will tell on trade.

Apr 9, 2017

The reason you don't generally hit runways
is that they are easy and inexpensive to
quickly fix (fill in and top)!

Apr 11, 2017

North Korea is looking for trouble.
If China decides to help, that would
be great. If not, we will solve the
problem without them! U.S.A.

Apr 12, 2017

Had a very good call last night with the
President of China concerning the
menace of North Korea.

Apr 13, 2017

Things will work out fine between the U.S.A.
and Russia. At the right time everyone will
come to their senses & there will
be lasting peace!

Apr 16, 2017

Why would I call China a currency
manipulator when they are working with
us on the North Korean problem?
We will see what happens!

Apr 17, 2017

The Fake Media (not Real Media) has gotten
even worse since the election.
Every story is badly slanted.
We have to hold them to the truth!

Apr 21, 2017

Another terrorist attack in Paris. The people
of France will not take much more of this.
Will have a big effect on
presidential election!

Apr 23, 2017

I am committed to keeping our air and water clean but always remember that economic growth enhances environmental protection. Jobs matter!

Apr 24, 2017

Eventually, but at a later date so we can get started early, Mexico will be paying, in some form, for the badly needed border wall.

Apr 25, 2017

The Wall is a very important tool in stopping drugs from pouring into our country and poisoning our youth (and many others)! If the wall is not built, which it will be, the drug situation will NEVER be fixed the way it should be! #BuildTheWall

Apr 25, 2017

Don't let the fake media tell you that
I have changed my position on the WALL.
It will get built and help stop drugs,
human trafficking etc.

Apr 28, 2017

I promise to rebuild our military
and secure our border.
Democrats want to shut down
the government. Politics!

Apr 29, 2017

North Korea disrespected the wishes of
China & its highly respected President
when it launched, though unsuccessfully,
a missile today. Bad!

May 6, 2017

Of course the Australians have better
healthcare than we do—everybody does.
ObamaCare is dead!
But our healthcare will soon be great.

May 9, 2017

The Russia-Trump collusion story is a
total hoax, when will this taxpayer
funded charade end?

May 10, 2017

J Comey lost the confidence of almost
everyone in Washington, Republican and
Democrat alike. When things calm down,
they will be thanking me!

May 10, 2017

The Democrats have said some of
the worst things about James Comey,
including the fact that he should be fired,
but now they play so sad!

May 11, 2017

Dems have been complaining for months &
months about Dir. Comey.
Now that he has been fired they
PRETEND to be aggrieved. Phony

May 12, 2017

James Comey better hope that there are
no "tapes" of our conversations before
he starts leaking to the press!

May 12, 2017

China just agreed that the U.S. will be allowed
to sell beef, and other major products,
into China once again. This is REAL news!

May 12, 2017

As a very active President with lots of
things happening, it is not possible
for my surrogates to stand at podium
with perfect accuracy!....

...Maybe the best thing to do would
be to cancel all future "press briefings"
and hand out written responses for
the sake of accuracy???

May 18, 2017

This is the single greatest witch hunt of a
politician in American history!

May 20, 2017

Getting ready for my big foreign trip.
Will be strongly protecting
American interests - that's what I like to do!

May 29, 2017

The Fake News Media works hard at
disparaging & demeaning my use of
social media because they don't want
America to hear the real story!

May 29, 2017

North Korea has shown great disrespect
for their neighbor, China, by shooting off
yet another ballistic missile ...
but China is trying hard!

May 30, 2017

⌐ Despite the constant
negative press covfefe ⌐

May 31, 2017

⌐ Who can figure out the true meaning of
"covfefe" ??? Enjoy! ⌐

Jun 1, 2017

Crooked Hillary Clinton now blames
everybody but herself, refuses to say
she was a terrible candidate. Hits Facebook
& even Dems & DNC.

Jun 4, 2017

At least 7 dead and 48 wounded in
terror attack and Mayor of London says
there is "no reason to be alarmed!"

Jun 4, 2017

We must stop being politically correct
and get down to the business of security
for our people. If we don't get smart
it will only get worse

Jun 4, 2017

Do you notice we are not having a
gun debate right now? That's because
they used knives and a truck!

Jun 5, 2017

People, the lawyers and the courts can
call it whatever they want,
but I am calling it what we need and
what it is, a TRAVEL BAN!

Jun 6, 2017

The FAKE MSM is working so hard
trying to get me not to use Social Media.
They hate that I can get the honest
and unfiltered message out.

Jun 9, 2017

Despite so many false statements and lies,
total and complete vindication... and WOW,
Comey is a leaker!

Jun 11, 2017

I believe the James Comey leaks will be
far more prevalent than anyone ever thought
possible. Totally illegal? Very 'cowardly!'

Jun 13, 2017

The Fake News Media has never been
so wrong or so dirty. Purposely incorrect
stories and phony sources to meet their
agenda of hate. Sad!

Jun 13, 2017

Well, as predicted, the 9th Circuit did it again -
Ruled against the TRAVEL BAN
at such a dangerous time in the
history of our country. S.C.

Jun 15, 2017

They made up a phony collusion
with the Russians story, found zero proof,
so now they go for obstruction of justice
on the phony story. Nice

Jun 16, 2017

Crooked H destroyed phones w/ hammer,
'bleached' emails, & had husband meet
w/AG days before she was cleared- &
they talk about obstruction?

Jun 16, 2017

The Fake News Media hates when
I use what has turned out to be my
very powerful Social Media - over
100 million people! I can go around them

Jun 16, 2017

Despite the phony Witch Hunt going on in America, the economic & jobs numbers are great. Regulations way down, jobs and enthusiasm way up!

Jun 16, 2017

I am being investigated for firing the FBI Director by the man who told me to fire the FBI Director! Witch Hunt

Jun 16, 2017

After 7 months of investigations & committee hearings about my "collusion with the Russians," nobody has been able to show any proof. Sad!

Jun 17, 2017

Back from Miami where my Cuban/American friends are very happy with what I signed today. Another campaign promise that I did not forget!

Jun 21, 2017

While I greatly appreciate the efforts of
President Xi & China to help with
North Korea, it has not worked out.
At least I know China tried!

Jun 22, 2017

Former Homeland Security Advisor
Jeh Johnson is latest top intelligence official
to state there was no grand scheme
between Trump & Russia.

Jun 22, 2017

By the way, if Russia was working
so hard on the 2016 Election, it all
took place during the Obama Admin.
Why didn't they stop them?

Jun 23, 2017

With all of the recently reported electronic surveillance, intercepts, unmasking and illegal leaking of information, I have no idea...

...whether there are "tapes" or recordings of my conversations with James Comey, but I did not make, and do not have, any such recordings.

Jun 23, 2017

I certainly hope the Democrats do not force Nancy P out. That would be very bad for the Republican Party - and please let Cryin' Chuck stay!

Jun 23, 2017

I've helped pass and signed 38 Legislative Bills, mostly with no Democratic support, and gotten rid of massive amounts of regulations. Nice!

Jun 23, 2017

Mexico was just ranked the
second deadliest country in the world,
after only Syria. Drug trade is largely the cause.
We will BUILD THE WALL!

Jun 24, 2017

Just out: The Obama Administration
knew far in advance of November 8th
about election meddling by Russia.
Did nothing about it. WHY?

Jun 25, 2017

Hillary Clinton colluded with the
Democratic Party in order to beat
Crazy Bernie Sanders. Is she allowed
to so collude? Unfair to Bernie!

Jun 25, 2017

MAKE AMERICA GREAT AGAIN!

Jun 25, 2017

Hillary Clinton colluded with the
Democratic Party in order to beat
Crazy Bernie Sanders. Is she allowed to so
collude? Unfair to Bernie!

Jun 26, 2017

The Democrats have become nothing but
OBSTRUCTIONISTS, they have no policies
or ideas. All they do is delay and complain.
They own ObamaCare!

Jun 27, 2017

So they caught Fake News CNN cold,
but what about NBC, CBS & ABC?
What about the failing @nytimes &
@washingtonpost? They are all Fake News!

Jun 27, 2017

Great day for America's future Security and
Safety, courtesy of the U.S. Supreme Court.
I will keep fighting for the
American people, & WIN!

Aug 1, 2017

Only the Fake News Media and
Trump enemies want me to stop using
Social Media (110 million people).
Only way for me to get the truth out!

Aug 1, 2017

"Corporations have NEVER made as much
money as they are making now."
Thank you Stuart Varney @foxandfriends
Jobs are starting to roar, watch!

Aug 3, 2017

I love the White House, one of the most
beautiful buildings (homes) I have ever seen.
But Fake News said I called it a dump -
TOTALLY UNTRUE

Aug 3, 2017

Our relationship with Russia is at an all-time
& very dangerous low.
You can thank Congress, the same people
that can't even give us HCare!

Aug 6, 2017

The United Nations Security Council
just voted 15-0 to sanction North Korea.
China and Russia voted with us.
Very big financial impact!

Aug 7, 2017

Never in U.S.history has anyone lied or
defrauded voters like
Senator Richard Blumenthal. He told stories
about his Vietnam battles and....

...conquests, how brave he was, and it was all a
lie. He cried like a baby and
begged for forgiveness like a child.
Now he judges collusion?

Aug 8, 2017

I think Senator Blumenthal should take
a nice long vacation in Vietnam,
where he lied about his service,
so he can at least say he was there

Aug 8, 2017

How much longer will the failing nytimes,
with its big losses and massiven unfunded
liability (and non-existent sources),
remain in business?

Aug 9, 2017

My first order as President was to
renovate and modernize our nuclear arsenal.
It is now far stronger and more powerful
than ever before....

...Hopefully we will never have to use
this power, but there will never be a time
that we are not the most powerful nation
in the world!

Aug 11, 2017

Military solutions are now fully in place,
locked and loaded,should North Korea act
unwisely. Hopefully Kim Jong Un
will find another path!

Aug 13, 2017

We ALL must be united & condemn
all that hate stands for. There is no place
for this kind of violence in America.
Lets come together as one!

Aug 14, 2017

Now that Ken Frazier of Merck Pharma has
resigned from President's Manufacturing
Council, he will have more time to
LOWER RIPOFF DRUG PRICES!

Aug 16, 2017

MAKE AMERICA GREAT AGAIN!

Aug 16, 2017

Kim Jong Un of North Korea made a
very wise and well reasoned decision.
The alternative would have been both
catastrophic and unacceptable!

Aug 17, 2017

Sad to see the history and culture of
our great country being ripped apart
with the removal of our beautiful statues
and monuments. You.....

...can't change history, but you can learn
from it. Robert E Lee, Stonewall Jackson -
who's next, Washington,
Jefferson? So foolish! Also...

...the beauty that is being taken out
of our cities, towns and parks will be
greatly missed and never able to be
comparably replaced!

Aug 17, 2017

The public is learning (even more so)
how dishonest the Fake News is.
They totally misrepresent what I say
about hate, bigotry etc. Shame!

Aug 18, 2017

The United States condemns the
terror attack in Barcelona, Spain,
and will do whatever is necessary to help.
Be tough & strong, we love you!

Aug 20, 2017

Our great country has been divided for
decades. Sometimes you need protest
in order to heal, & we will heal,
& be stronger than ever before!

Aug 20, 2017

Looks like many anti-police agitators
in Boston. Police are looking tough and smart!
Thank you.

Aug 24, 2017

The Fake News is now
complaining about my different types of
back to back speeches. Well, there was
Afghanistan (somber), the big Rally.....

..(enthusiastic, dynamic and fun) and the
American Legion - V.A. (respectful and strong).
Too bad the Dems have no one
who can change tones!

Aug 26, 2017

Just arrived at Camp David where
I am closely watching the path and doings of
Hurricane Harvey, as it strengthens to a
Category 3. BE SAFE!

Aug 26, 2017

I am pleased to inform you that
I have just granted a full Pardon to 85 year old
American patriot Sheriff Joe Arpaio.
He kept Arizona safe!

Aug 27, 2017

With Mexico being one of the highest crime
Nations in the world, we must have
THE WALL. Mexico will pay for it
through reimbursement/other.

Aug 30, 2017

The U.S. has been talking to North Korea, and
paying them extortion money, for 25 years.
Talking is not the answer!

Aug 30, 2017

After reading the false reporting and even
ferocious anger in some dying magazines, it
makes me wonder, WHY? All I want to do
is #MAGA!

Sep 1, 2017

Wow, looks like James Comey exonerated
Hillary Clinton long before the
investigation was over ... and so much more.
A rigged system!

Sep 1, 2017

General John Kelly is doing a great job
as Chief of Staff. I could not be happier or
more impressed - and this Administration
continues to..

...get things done at a record clip. Many big
decisions to be made over the coming days and
weeks. AMERICA FIRST!

Sep 3, 2017

South Korea is finding, as I have told them,
that their talk of appeasement with
North Korea will not work,
they only understand one thing!

Sep 3, 2017

North Korea has conducted a major
Nuclear Test. Their words and actions
continue to be very hostile and dangerous
to the United States.....

Sep 5, 2017

Big week coming up!

Sep 8, 2017

Hurricane Irma is of epic proportion,
perhaps bigger than we have ever seen.
Be safe and get out of its way,if possible.
Federal G is ready!

Sep 12, 2017

Fascinating to watch people writing books
and major articles about me and yet they
know nothing about me & have zero access.
#FAKE NEWS!

Sep 14, 2017

The "deplorables" came back to haunt
Hillary.They expressed their feelings loud
and clear. She spent big money but,
in the end, had no game!

Sep 14, 2017

The WALL, which is already under
construction in the form of new renovation
of old and existing fences and walls,
will continue to be built.

Sep 15, 2017

ESPN is paying a really big price for its
politics (and bad programming).
People are dumping it in RECORD numbers.
Apologize for untruth!

Sep 15, 2017

Spoke to President of Mexico to give
condolences on terrible earthquake.
Unable to reach for 3 days b/c of his
cell phone reception at site.

Sep 15, 2017

Another attack in London by a loser terrorist.
These are sick and demented people who
were in the sights of Scotland Yard.
Must be proactive!

Sep 15, 2017

The travel ban into the United States
should be far larger, tougher and more
specific-but stupidly, that would not be
politically correct!

Sep 17, 2017

I spoke with President Moon of
South Korea last night. Asked him how
Rocket Man is doing. Long gas lines
forming in North Korea. Too bad!

Sep 19, 2017

Big day at the United Nations - many good
things, and some tricky ones, happening.
We have a great team.
Big speech at 10:00 A.M.

Sep 20, 2017

I was saddened to see how bad the ratings
were on the Emmys last night - the worst
ever. Smartest people of them all are the
"DEPLORABLES."

Sep 20, 2017

After allowing North Korea to research and build Nukes while Secretary of State (Bill C also), Crooked Hillary now criticizes.

Sep 20, 2017

Rand Paul is a friend of mine but he is such a negative force when it comes to fixing healthcare. Graham-Cassidy Bill is GREAT! Ends Ocare!

Sep 22, 2017

The greatest influence over our election was the Fake News Media "screaming" for Crooked Hillary Clinton. Next, she was a bad candidate!

Sep 22, 2017

Kim Jong Un of North Korea, who is obviously a madman who doesn't mind starving or killing his people, will be tested like never before!

Sep 23, 2017

Going to the White House is
considered a great honor for a
championship team. Stephen Curry is
hesitating, therefore invitation is withdrawn!

Sep 24, 2017

If a player wants the privilege of
making millions of dollars in the NFL,
or other leagues, he or she should not
be allowed to disrespect....

...our Great American Flag (or Country)
and should stand for the National Anthem.
If not, YOU'RE FIRED.
Find something else to do!

Sep 24, 2017

...NFL attendance and ratings are
WAY DOWN. Boring games yes,
but many stay away because they
love our country. League should back U.S.

Sep 24, 2017

Iran just test-fired a Ballistic Missile
capable of reaching Israel. They are
also working with North Korea.
Not much of an agreement we have!

Sep 24, 2017

Just heard Foreign Minister of
North Korea speak at U.N. If he echoes
thoughts of Little Rocket Man,
they won't be around much longer!

Sep 26, 2017

The booing at the NFL football game
last night, when the entire Dallas team
dropped to its knees, was loudest
I have ever heard. Great anger

Sep 29, 2017

...The fact is that Puerto Rico has been
destroyed by two hurricanes.
Big decisions will have to be made
as to the cost of its rebuilding!

Oct 2, 2017

I told Rex Tillerson, our wonderful Secretary of State, that he is wasting his time trying to negotiate with Little Rocket Man...

...Save your energy Rex, we'll do what has to be done!

Oct 2, 2017

Being nice to Rocket Man hasn't worked in
25 years, why would it work now?
Clinton failed, Bush failed, and
Obama failed. I won't fail.

Oct 2, 2017

My warmest condolences and
sympathies to the victims and
families of the terrible
Las Vegas shooting. God bless you!

Oct 5, 2017

Rex Tillerson never threatened to resign.
This is Fake News put out by @NBCNews.
Low news and reporting standards.
No verification from me.

Oct 8, 2017

Presents and their administrations
have been talking to North Korea for 25 years,
agreements made and massive amounts of
money paid......

...hasn't worked, agreements violated
before the ink was dry,
makings fools of U.S. negotiators.
Sorry, but only one thing will work!

Oct 9, 2017

I asked @VP Pence to leave stadium
if any players kneeled, disrespecting
our country. I am proud of him and @
SecondLady Karen.

Oct 9, 2017

...Hence, I would fully expect Corker
to be a negative voice and stand
in the way of our great agenda.
Didn't have the guts to run!

Oct 11, 2017

The Fake News is at it again,
this time trying to hurt one of the
finest people I know, General John Kelly,
by saying he will soon be.....

...fired. This story is totally made up by the
dishonest media. The Chief is
doing a FANTASTIC job for me and,
more importantly, for the USA!

Oct 12, 2017

The Fake News Is going all out in order to
demean and denigrate! Such hatred!

Oct 13, 2017

Hard to believe that the Democrats,
who have gone so far LEFT that they are
no longer recognizable, are fighting
so hard for Sanctuary crime

Oct 14, 2017

Starting to develop a much better relationship with Pakistan and its leaders. I want to thank them for their cooperation on many fronts.

Oct 18, 2017

As it has turned out, James Comey lied and leaked and totally protected Hillary Clinton. He was the best thing that ever happened to her!

Oct 18, 2017

Democrat Congresswoman totally fabricated what I said to the wife of a soldier who died in action (and I have proof). Sad!

Oct 19, 2017

Workers of firm involved with
the discredited and Fake Dossier take the 5th.
Who paid for it, Russia,
the FBI or the Dems (or all)?

Oct 22, 2017

Crooked Hillary Clinton spent hundreds
of millions of dollars more on
Presidential Election than I did.
Facebook was on her side, not mine!

Oct 25, 2017

The meeting with Republican Senators
yesterday, outside of Flake and Corker,
was a love fest with standing ovations and
great ideas for USA!

Oct 30, 2017

All of this "Russia" talk right when
the Republicans are making their
big push for historic Tax Cuts & Reform.
Is this coincidental? NOT!

Nov 3, 2017

My Twitter account was taken down
for 11 minutes by a rogue employee.
I guess the word must finally be
getting out-and having an impact.

Nov 3, 2017

Pocahontas just stated that the Democrats,
lead by the legendary Crooked
Hillary Clinton, rigged the Primaries!
Lets go FBI & Justice Dept.

Nov 4, 2017

Would very much appreciate
Saudi Arabia doing their IPO of
Aramco with the New York Stock Exchange.
Important to the United States!

Nov 10, 2017

I don't blame China, I blame the incompetence
of past Admins for allowing China
to take advantage of the U.S. on trade leading up
to a point where the U.S. is losing $100's
of billions. How can you blame China
for taking advantage of people
that had no clue? I would've done same!

Nov 12, 2017

Why would Kim Jong-un insult me
by calling me "old," when I would
NEVER call him "short and fat?"
Oh well, I try so hard to be his friend -
and maybe someday that will happen!

Nov 12, 2017

When will all the haters and fools out there
realize that having a good relationship with
Russia is a good thing, not a bad thing.
There always playing politics - bad for our
country. I want to solve North Korea,
Syria, Ukraine, terrorism, and
Russia can greatly help!

Nov 15, 2017

While in the Philippines I was forced
to watch @CNN, which I have not done
in months, and again realized how bad,
and FAKE, it is. Loser!

Nov 17, 2017

The Al Frankenstien picture is really bad,
speaks a thousand words. Where do his
hands go in pictures 2, 3, 4, 5 & 6 while she
sleeps? ...... And to think that just last week he
was lecturing anyone who would listen
about sexual harassment and
respect for women. Lesley Stahl tape?

Nov 20, 2017

Now that the three basketball players
are out of China and saved from years in jail,
LaVar Ball, the father of LiAngelo,
is unaccepting of what I did for his son
and that shoplifting is no big deal.
I should have left them in jail!

Nov 22, 2017

It wasn't the White House, it wasn't the State
Department, it wasn't father LaVar's
so-called people on the ground in
China that got his son out of a
long term prison sentence - IT WAS ME.
Too bad! LaVar is just a poor man's version of
Don King, but without the hair. Just think..

...LaVar, you could have spent the
next 5 to 10 years during Thanksgiving
with your son in China, but no NBA contract
to support you. But remember LaVar,
shoplifting is NOT a little thing.
It's a really big deal, especially in China.
Ungrateful fool!

Nov 25, 2017

Time Magazine called to say that
I was PROBABLY going to be named
"Man (Person) of the Year," like last year,
but I would have to agree to an interview
and a major photo shoot. I said probably
is no good and took a pass. Thanks anyway!

Nov 28, 2017

We should have a contest as to which
of the Networks, plus CNN and not
including Fox, is the most dishonest,
corrupt and/or distorted in its
political coverage of your
favorite President (me).
They are all bad. Winner to receive the
FAKE NEWS TROPHY!

Nov 29, 2017

Melania, our great and very hard working
First Lady, who truly loves what
she is doing, always thought that
"if you run, you will win." She would tell
everyone that, "no doubt, he will win."
I also felt I would win
(or I would not have run) -
and Country is doing great!

Dec 3, 2017

I had to fire General Flynn because
he lied to the Vice President and the FBI.
He has pled guilty to those lies.
It is a shame because his actions
during the transition were lawful.
There was nothing to hide!

Dec 7, 2017

MAKE AMERICA GREAT AGAIN!

Dec 10, 2017

CNN'S slogan is CNN,
THE MOST TRUSTED NAME IN NEWS.
Everyone knows this is not true,
that this could, in fact, be a fraud on the
American Public. There are many outlets
that are far more trusted than
Fake News CNN. Their slogan should be
CNN, THE LEAST TRUSTED NAME
IN NEWS!

Dec 12, 2017

Another false story, this time in the Failing @
nytimes, that I watch 4-8 hours of
television a day -Wrong! Also, I seldom,
if ever, watch CNN or MSNBC,
both of which I consider Fake News.
I never watch Don Lemon, who I once called
the "dumbest man on television!"
Bad Reporting.

Dec 14, 2017

Wow, more than 90% of
Fake News Media coverage of me is
negative, with numerous forced retractions
of untrue stories. Hence my use of
Social Media, the only way
to get the truth out. Much of Mainstream
Media has become a joke! @foxandfriends

Dec 25, 2017

People are proud to be saying
Merry Christmas again. I am proud to
have led the charge against the assault of our
cherished and beautiful phrase.
MERRY CHRISTMAS!!!!!

Dec 26, 2017

I hope everyone is having a great Christmas,
then tomorrow it's back to work in order
to Make America Great Again
(which is happening faster
than anyone anticipated)!

Dec 29, 2017

In the East, it could be the
COLDEST New Year's Eve on record.
Perhaps we could use a little bit of that
good old Global Warming that our Country,
but not other countries, was going to pay
TRILLIONS OF DOLLARS to
protect against. Bundle up!

2018

Jan 3, 2018

I will be announcing
THE MOST DISHONEST & CORRUPT
MEDIA AWARDS OF THE YEAR
on Monday at 5:00 o'clock. Subjects will cover
Dishonesty & Bad Reporting in
various categories from the Fake News Media.
Stay tuned!

Jan 3, 2018

North Korean Leader Kim Jong Un
just stated that the "Nuclear Button is on his
desk at all times." Will someone from
his depleted and food starved regime please
inform him that I too have a Nuclear Button,
but it is a much bigger & more powerful one
than his, and my Button works!

Jan 4, 2018

MAKE AMERICA GREAT AGAIN!

Jan 5, 2018

I authorized Zero access to White House
(actually turned him down many times)
for author of phony book! In ever spoke
to him for book. Full of lies,
misrepresentations and sources that
don't exist. Look at this guy's past and watch
what happens to him and Sloppy Steve!

Jan 6, 2018

Now that Russian collusion, after
one year of intense study, has proven to be a
total hoax on the American public,
the Democrats and their lapdogs, the
Fake News Mainstream Media, are taking out
the old Ronald Reagan playbook and
screaming mental stability and intelligence…..

….Actually, throughout my life,
my two greatest assets have been
mental stability and being, like, really smart.
Crooked Hillary Clinton also played these cards
very hard and, as everyone knows,
went down in flames. I went from VERY
successful businessman, to top T.V. Star…..

….to President of the United States
(on my first try). I think that would qualify
as not smart, but genius …. and a very stable
genius at that!

Jan 12, 2018

Reason I canceled my trip to London is
that I am not a big fan of the
Obama Administration having sold
perhaps the best located and finest embassy
in London for "peanuts," only to build a
new one in an off location for
1.2 billion dollars. Bad deal.
Wanted me to cut ribbon-NO!

Jan 14, 2018

So much Fake News is being reported.
They don't even try to get it right,
or correct it when they are wrong.
They promote the Fake Book of a mentally
deranged author, who knowingly writes false
information. The Mainstream Media is
crazed that WE won the election!

Jan 14, 2018

AMERICA FIRST!

Jan 18, 2018

The Wall is the Wall, it has never changed
or evolved from the first day I conceived of it.
Parts will be, of necessity, see through and
it was never intended to be built in areas
where there is natural protection such as
mountains, wastelands or tough rivers
or water.....

Jan 21, 2018

Beautiful weather all over our great country,
a perfect day for all Women to March.
Get out there now to celebrate the historic
milestones and unprecedented
economic success and wealth creation that has
taken place over the last 12 months.
Lowest female unemployment in 18 years!

Jan 23, 2018

In one of the biggest stories in a long time, the FBI now says it is missing five months worth of lovers Strzok-Page texts, perhaps 50,000, and all in prime time. Wow!

Jan 24, 2018

Where are the 50,000 important text messages between FBI lovers Lisa Page and Peter Strzok? Blaming Samsung!

Feb 18, 2018

Finally, Liddle' Adam Schiff, the leakin' monster of no control, is now blaming the Obama Administration for Russian meddling in the 2016 Election. He is finally right about something. Obama was President, knew of the threat, and did nothing. Thank you Adam!

Feb 18, 2018

I never said Russia did not meddle in the election, I said "it may be Russia, or China or another country or group, or it may be a 400 pound genius sitting in bed and playing with his computer." The Russian "hoax" was that the Trump campaign colluded with Russia - it never did!

Mar 2, 2018

Good (Great) meeting in the
Oval Office tonight with the NRA!

Mar 7, 2018

Lowest rated Oscars in HISTORY. Problem
is, we don't have Stars anymore - except your
President (just kidding, of course)!

Mar 22, 2018

Crazy Joe Biden is trying to act like a
tough guy. Actually, he is weak,
both mentally and physically, and yet
he threatens me, for the second time,
with physical assault. He doesn't know me,
but he would go down fast and hard,
crying all the way. Don't threaten people Joe!

Apr 2, 2018

Mexico is doing very little,
if not NOTHING, at stopping people
from flowing into Mexico through their
Southern Border, and then into the U.S.
They laugh at our dumb immigration laws.
They must stop the big drug and people flows,
or I will stop their cash cow, NAFTA.
NEED WALL!

Apr 8, 2018

President Xi and I will always be friends,
no matter what happens with our
dispute on trade. China will take down its
Trade Barriers because it is the right thing
to do. Taxes will become Reciprocal
& a deal will be made on
Intellectual Property.
Great future for both countries!

Apr 8, 2018

Fire at Trump Tower is out. Very confined
(well built building). Firemen (and women)
did a great job. THANK YOU!

Apr 8, 2018

If President Obama had crossed his stated
Red Line In The Sand, the Syrian disaster
would have ended long ago!
Animal Assad would have been history!

Apr 11, 2018

Russia vows to shoot down any and all missiles fired at Syria. Get ready Russia, because they will be coming, nice and new and "smart!" You shouldn't be partners with a Gas Killing Animal who kills his people and enjoys it!

Apr 13, 2018

James Comey is a proven LEAKER & LIAR. Virtually everyone in Washington thought he should be fired for the terrible job he did-until he was, in fact, fired. He leaked CLASSIFIED information, for which he should be prosecuted. He lied to Congress under OATH. He is a weak and.....

....untruthful slime ball who was, as time has proven, a terrible Director of the FBI. His handling of the Crooked Hillary Clinton case, and the events surrounding it, will go down as one of the worst "botch jobs" of history. It was my great honor to fire James Comey!

Apr 14, 2018

A perfectly executed strike last night.
Thank you to France and the United Kingdom
for their wisdom and the power of their fine
Military. Could not have had a better result.
Mission Accomplished!

Apr 15, 2018

The Syrian raid was so perfectly carried out,
with such precision, that the only way the
Fake News Media could demean was
by my use of the term "Mission Accomplished."
Ik new they would seize on this but felt
it is such a great Military term,
it should be brought back. Use often!

Apr 17, 2018

Employment is up, Taxes are DOWN. Enjoy!

Apr 18, 2018

Pastor Andrew Brunson, a fine gentleman and
Christian leader in the United States,
is on trial and being persecuted in Turkey
for no reason. They call him a Spy,
but I am more a Spy than he is.
Hopefully he will be allowed to
come home to his beautiful family
where he belongs!

Apr 19, 2018

Best wishes to Prime Minister @Netanyahu
and all of the people of Israel on the
70th Anniversary of your Great Independence.
We have no better friends anywhere.
Looking forward to moving our Embassy
to Jerusalem next month!

Apr 22, 2018

Sleepy Eyes Chuck Todd of Fake News
NBC just stated that we have given up
so much in our negotiations with
North Korea, and they have given up
nothing. Wow, we haven't given up anything
& they have agreed to denuclearization
(so great for World), site closure,
& no more testing!

Apr 23, 2018

A complete Witch Hunt!

Apr 27, 2018

After a furious year of missile launches
and Nuclear testing, a historic meeting
between North and South Korea is
now taking place. Good things are happening,
but only time will tell!

May 3, 2018

Our great financial team is in China
trying to negotiate a level playing field on trade!
I look forward to being with President Xi
in the not too distant future. We will always
have a good (great) relationship!

May 4, 2018

JUST OUT: 3.9% Unemployment. 4% is Broken! In the meantime, WITCH HUNT!

May 7, 2018

The 13 Angry Democrats in charge of the Russian Witch Hunt are starting to find out that there is a Court System in place that actually protects people from injustice... and just wait 'till the Courts get to see your unrevealed Conflicts of Interest!

May 14, 2018

So sad to see the Terror Attack in Paris. At some point countries will have to open their eyes & see what is really going on. This kind of sickness & hatred is not compatible with a loving, peaceful, & successful country! Changes to our thought process on terror must be made.

May 19, 2018

America is blessed with extraordinary
energy abundance, including more than
250 years worth of beautiful clean coal.
We have ended the war on coal, and
will continue to work to promote
American energy dominance!

May 23, 2018

SPYGATE could be one of the
biggest political scandals in history!

May 23, 2018

WITCH HUNT!

May 29, 2018

The Fake Mainstream Media has,
from the time I announced I was running for
President, run the most highly sophisticated &
dishonest Disinformation Campaign
in the history of politics. No matter how well
WE do, they find fault. But the
forgotten men & women WON,
I'm President!

May 29, 2018

Sorry, I've got to start focusing my
energy on North Korea Nuclear,
bad Trade Deals, VA Choice, the Economy,
rebuilding the Military, and so much more,
and not on the Rigged Russia Witch Hunt
that should be investigating Clinton/Russia/
FBI/Justice/Obama/Convey/Lynch etc.

May 29, 2018

Why aren't the 13 Angry and heavily conflicted
Democrats investigating the totally
Crooked Campaign of totally Crooked
Hillary Clinton. It's a Rigged Witch Hunt,
that's why! Ask them if they enjoyed her after
election celebration!

Jun 3, 2018

The United States must, at long last, be treated fairly on Trade. If we charge a country ZERO to sell their goods, and they charge us 25, 50 or even 100 percent to sell ours, it is UNFAIR and can no longer be tolerated. That is not Free or Fair Trade, it is Stupid Trade!

Jun 6, 2018

Wow, Strzok-Page, the incompetent &
corrupt FBI lovers, have texts referring to a
counter-intelligence operation into the Trump
Campaign dating way back to December, 2015.
SPYGATE is in full force! Is the Mainstream
Media interested yet? Big stuff!

Jun 7, 2018

When and where will all of the
many conflicts of interest be listed by the
13 Angry Democrats (plus) working on the
Witch Hunt Hoax. There has never been
a group of people on a case so biased or
conflicted. It is all a Democrat Excuse for
LOSING the Election. Where is the server?

Jun 8, 2018

When will people start saying, "thank you,
Mr. President, for firing James Comey?"

Jun 10, 2018

PM Justin Trudeau of Canada acted so
meek and mild during our @G7 meetings
only to give a news conference after I left
saying that, "US Tariffs were kind of insulting"
and he "will not be pushed around."
Very dishonest & weak. Our Tariffs are in
response to his of 270% on dairy!

Jun 11, 2018

Fair Trade is now to be called Fool Trade
if it is not Reciprocal. According to a Canada
release, they make almost 100 Billion Dollars
in Trade with U.S. (guess they were bragging
and got caught!). Minimum is 17B.
Tax Dairy from us at 270%.
Then Justin acts hurt when called out!

Jun 13, 2018

The World has taken a big step back from
potential Nuclear catastrophe!
No more rocket launches,
nuclear testing or research!
The hostages are back home
with their families. Thank you to
Chairman Kim, our day together was historic!

Jun 13, 2018

Robert De Niro, a very Low IQ individual,
has received too many shots to the head
by real boxers in movies. I watched him
last night and truly believe he may be
"punch-drunk." I guess he doesn't...

...realize the economy is the best it's ever been
with employment being at an all time high,
and many companies pouring back into
our country. Wake up Punchy!

Jun 15, 2018

Now that I am back from Singapore,
where we had a great result with respect to
North Korea, the thought process must sadly go
back to the Witch Hunt, always
remembering that there was
No Collusion and No Obstruction
of the fabricated No Crime.

Jun 16, 2018

My supporters are the smartest, strongest,
most hard working and most loyal that
we have seen in our countries history.
It is a beautiful thing to watch as we win
elections and gather support from all over
the country. As we get stronger, so does
our country. Best numbers ever!

Jun 16, 2018

Democrats can fix their forced
family breakup at the Border by working
with Republicans on new legislation, for a
change! This is why we need more Republicans
elected in November. Democrats are good
at only three things, High Taxes,
High Crime and Obstruction. Sad!

Jun 18, 2018

Why was the FBI's sick loser,
Peter Strzok, working on the totally discredited
Mueller team of 13 Angry &
Conflicted Democrats, when Strzok
was giving Crooked Hillary a free pass yet telling
his lover, lawyer Lisa Page, that "we'll stop"
Trump from becoming President? Witch Hunt!

Jun 19, 2018

I can't think of something more concerning
than a law enforcement officer suggesting that
their going to use their powers to affect an
election!" Inspector General Horowitz on
what was going on with numerous people
regarding my election. A Rigged Witch Hunt!

Jun 22, 2018

"I REALLY DON'T CARE, DO U?"
written on the back of Melania's jacket,
refers to the Fake News Media.
Melania has learned how dishonest they are,
and she truly no longer cares!

Jun 25, 2018

.@jimmyfallon is now whimpering to
all that he did the famous "hair show"
with me (where he seriously messed up my hair),
& that he would have now done it differently
because it is said to have "humanized"
me-he is taking heat. He called & said
"monster ratings." Be a man Jimmy!

Jun 25, 2018

The Red Hen Restaurant should focus more
on cleaning its filthy canopies, doors and
windows (badly needs a paint job)
rather than refusing to serve a fine person
like Sarah Huckabee Sanders.
I always had a rule, if a restaurant is dirty
on the outside, it is dirty on the inside!

Jun 26, 2018

The face of the Democrats is now
Maxine Waters who, together with
Nancy Pelosi, have established a fine
leadership team. They should always
stay together and lead the Democrats,
who want Open Borders and
Unlimited Crime, well into the future ....
and pick Crooked Hillary for Pres.

Jun 26, 2018

Why is Senator Mark Warner (D-VA),
perhaps in a near drunken state,
claiming he has information that only he and
Bob Mueller, the leader of the 13 Angry
Democrats on a Witch Hunt, knows?
Isn't this highly illegal. Is it being investigated?

Jun 27, 2018

Congratulations to Maxine Waters,
whose crazy rants have made her,
together with Nancy Pelosi, the unhinged
FACE of the Democrat Party.
Together, they will Make America
Weak Again! But have no fear,
America is now stronger than ever before,
and I'm not going anywhere!

Jun 27, 2018

HOUSE REPUBLICANS SHOULD PASS
THE STRONG BUT FAIR IMMIGRATION
BILL, KNOWN AS GOODLATTE II, IN
THEIR AFTERNOON VOTE TODAY, EVEN
THOUGH THE DEMS WON'T LET IT PASS
IN THE SENATE. PASSAGE WILL SHOW
THAT WE WANT STRONG BORDERS
& SECURITY WHILE THE DEMS WANT
OPEN BORDERS = CRIME. WIN!

Jun 27, 2018

SUPREME COURT UPHOLDS TRUMP
TRAVEL BAN. Wow!

Jul 3, 2018

Crazy Maxine Waters, said by some to
be one of the most corrupt people in politics,
is rapidly becoming, together with
Nancy Pelosi, the FACE of the Democrat Party.
Her ranting and raving, even referring to
herself as a wounded animal, will make
people flee the Democrats!

Jul 4, 2018

After having written many best selling books, and somewhat priding myself on my ability to write, it should be noted that the Fake News constantly likes to pore over my tweets looking for a mistake. I capitalize certain words only for emphasis, not b/c they should be capitalized!

Jul 8, 2018

The Rigged Witch Hunt, originally headed by FBI lover boy Peter S (for one year) & now, 13 Angry Democrats, should look into the missing DNC Server, Crooked Hillary's illegally deleted Emails, the Pakistani Fraudster, Uranium One, Podesta & so much more. It's a Democrat Con Job!

Jul 11, 2018

I am on Air Force One flying to NATO
and hear reports that the FBI lovers,
Peter Strzok and Lisa Page are getting
cold feet on testifying about the
Rigged Witch Hunt headed by
13 Angry Democrats and people that
worked for Obama for 8 years. Total disgrace!

Jul 18, 2018

Some people HATE the fact that
I got along well with President Putin of Russia.
They would rather go to war than see this.
It's called Trump Derangement Syndrome!

Jul 18, 2018

So many people at the higher ends of
intelligence loved my press conference
performance in Helsinki. Putin and
I discussed many important subjects at
our earlier meeting. We got along well which truly
bothered many haters who wanted to
see a boxing match. Big results will come!

Jul 19, 2018

The Fake News Media is going Crazy!
They make up stories without any backup,
sources or proof. Many of the stories written
about me, and the good people surrounding me,
are total fiction. Problem is, when you complain
you just give them more publicity.
But I'll complain anyway!

11:24 pm | Jul 23, 2018

To Iranian President Rouhani:
NEVER, EVER THREATEN THE
UNITED STATES AGAIN OR YOU WILL
SUFFER CONSEQUENCES THE LIKES
OF WHICH FEW THROUGHOUT
HISTORY HAVE EVER SUFFERED
BEFORE. WE ARE NO LONGER A
COUNTRY THAT WILL STAND FOR
YOUR DEMENTED WORDS OF
VIOLENCE & DEATH. BE CAUTIOUS!

Jul 24, 2018

Tariffs are the greatest! Either a country which has treated the United States unfairly on Trade negotiates a fair deal, or it gets hit with Tariffs. It's as simple as that - and everybody's talking! Remember, we are the "piggy bank" that's being robbed. All will be Great!

Aug 2, 2018

Thank you to Chairman Kim Jong Un
for keeping your word & starting the process of
sending home the remains of our great
and beloved missing fallen! I am not at all
surprised that you took this kind action.
Also, thank you for your nice letter -
I look forward to seeing you soon!

Aug 4, 2018

Lebron James was just interviewed
by the dumbest man on television,
Don Lemon. He made Lebron look smart,
which isn't easy to do. 1 like Mike!

Aug 9, 2018

RED WAVE!

Aug 10, 2018

Space Force all the way!

Aug 11, 2018

Democrats, please do not distance
yourselves from Nancy Pelosi.
She is a wonderful person whose ideas &
policies may be bad, but who should
definitely be given a 4th chance. She is trying
very hard & has every right to take down the
Democrat Party if she has veered too far left!

Wacky Omarosa, who got fired 3 times on the
Apprentice, now got fired for the last time.
She never made it, never will. She begged
me for a job, tears in her eyes, I said Ok.
People in the White House hated her.
She was vicious, but not smart.
I would rarely see her but heard....

...really bad things. Nasty to people & would
constantly miss meetings & work.
When Gen. Kelly came on board he told me
she was a loser & nothing but problems.
I told him to try working it out, if possible,
because she only said GREAT things
about me - until she got fired!

When you give a crazed,
crying lowlife a break, and give her a job
at the White House, I guess it just
didn't work out. Good work
by General Kelly for quickly firing that dog!

Aug 14, 2018

Another terrorist attack in London ...
These animals are crazy and must be dealt with
through toughness and strength!

Aug 17, 2018

How does a politician, Cuomo,
known for pushing people and businesses
out of his state, not to mention having
the highest taxes in the U.S., survive making the
statement, WE'RE NOT GOING
TO MAKE AMERICA GREAT AGAIN,
IT WAS NEVER THAT GREAT?
Which section of the sentence is worse?

Aug 19, 2018

Study the late Joseph McCarthy,
because we are now in period with
Mueller and his gang that make
Joseph McCarthy look like a baby!
Rigged Witch Hunt!

Aug 21, 2018

A Blue Wave means Crime and Open Borders.
A Red Wave means Safety and Strength!

Aug 22, 2018

If anyone is looking for a good lawyer,
I would strongly suggest that you don't retain
the services of Michael Cohen!

Aug 25, 2018

Congratulations to new
Australian Prime Minister Scott Morrison.
There are no greater friends than the
United States and Australia!

Aug 27, 2018

Over 90% approval rating for your all time
favorite (I hope) President within the Republican
Party and 52% overall. This despite all of the
made up stories by the Fake News Media trying
endlessly to make me look as bad and evil as
possible. Look at the real villains please!

Aug 29, 2018

Big Election Wins last night!
The Republican Party will MAKE AMERICA
GREAT AGAIN! Actually, it is happening
faster than anybody thought possible! It is
morphing into KEEP AMERICA GREAT!

Sep 6, 2018

I'm draining the Swamp, and the Swamp is trying to fight back. Don't worry, we will win!

Sep 6, 2018

TREASON?

Sep 7, 2018

What was Nike thinking?

Sep 13, 2018

3000 people did not die in the
two hurricanes that hit Puerto Rico.
When I left the Island, AFTER the storm
had hit, they had anywhere from 6 to 18 deaths.
As time went by it did not go up by much.
Then, a long time later, they started to report
really large numbers, like 3000...

…..This was done by the Democrats in
order to make me look as bad as possible
when I was successfully raising Billions of
Dollars to help rebuild Puerto Rico.
If a person died for any reason, like old age,
just add them onto the list. Bad politics.
I love Puerto Rico!

Sep 17, 2018

Best economic numbers in decades.
If the Democrats take control, kiss your
newfound wealth goodbye!

Sep 25, 2018

Despite requests, I have no plans to
meet Iranian President Hassan Rouhani.
Maybe someday in the future. I am sure
he is an absolutely lovely man!

Oct 3, 2018

THE ONLY REASON TO VOTE
FOR A DEMOCRAT IS IF YOU'RE
TIRED OF WINNING!

Oct 4, 2018

Our country's great First Lady, Melania,
is doing really well in Africa.
The people love her, and she loves them!
It is a beautiful thing to see.

Oct 16, 2018

Federal Judge throws out Stormy Danials
lawsuit versus Trump. Trump is entitled to full
legal fees." @FoxNews Great, now I can go
after Horseface and her 3rd rate lawyer in the
Great State of Texas. She will confirm the letter
she signed! She knows nothing about me,
a total con!

Oct 16, 2018

Pocahontas (the bad version), sometimes
referred to as Elizabeth Warren, is getting
slammed. She took a bogus DNA test and it
showed that she may be 1/1024, far less than
the average American. Now Cherokee Nation
denies her, "DNA test is useless."
Even they don't want her. Phony!

Beto O'Rourke is a total lightweight
compared to Ted Cruz, and he comes
nowhere near representing the values and
desires of the people of the
Great State of Texas. He will never be
allowed to turn Texas into Venezuela!

Oct 20, 2018

When referring to the USA,
I will always capitalize the word Country!

Oct 22, 2018

Sadly, it looks like Mexico's Police and Military
are unable to stop the Caravan heading to the
Southern Border of the United States. Criminals
and unknown Middle Easterners are mixed in.
I have alerted Border Patrol and Military that
this is a National Emergy. Must change laws!

Oct 23, 2018

The Fake News Media has been
talking about recent approval ratings of me by
countries around the world, including
the European Union, as being very low....

....I say of course they're low - because for
the first time in 50 years I am making them pay a
big price for doing business with America.
Why should they like me? — But I still like them!

Nov 13, 2018

Emmanuel Macron suggests building its own army to protect Europe against the U.S., China and Russia. But it was Germany in World Wars One & Two - How did that work out for France? They were starting to learn German in Paris before the U.S. came along. Pay for NATO or not!

Nov 14, 2018

…...MAKE FRANCE GREAT AGAIN!

Dec 5, 2018

....I am a Tariff Man. When people or
countries come in to raid the great wealth of our
Nation, I want them to pay for the
privilege of doing so. It will always be the
best way to max out our economic power.
We are right now taking in $billions in Tariffs.
MAKE AMERICA RICH AGAIN

Dec 8, 2018

The Paris Agreement isn't working out
so well for Paris. Protests and riots all over
France. People do not want to pay large
sums of money, much to third world countries
(that are questionably run), in order to
maybe protect the environment. Chanting
"We Want Trump!" Love France.

Dec 8, 2018

Mike Pompeo is doing a great job, I am very
proud of him. His predecessor, Rex Tillerson,
didn't have the mental capacity needed. He was
dumb as a rock and I couldn't get rid of
him fast enough. He was lazy as hell.
Now it is a whole new ballgame,
great spirit at State!

Dec 16, 2018

Never in the history of our Country has the
"press" been more dishonest than it is today.
Stories that should be good, are bad.
Stories that should be bad, are horrible.
Many stories, like with the REAL story on
Russia, Clinton & the DNC,
seldom get reported. Too bad!

Dec 17, 2018

So where are all the missing Text messages
between fired FBI agents Peter S and
the lovely Lisa Page, his lover.
Just reported that they have been erased and
wiped clean. What an outrage as the totally
compromised and conflicted Witch Hunt
moves ever so slowly forward. Want them!

Dec 19, 2018

The Democrats, are saying loud and clear that
they do not want to build a Concrete Wall -
but we are not building a Concrete Wall,
we are building artistically designed steel slats,
so that you can easily see through it....

Dec 21, 2018

The Democrats are trying to belittle
the concept of a Wall, calling it old fashioned.
The fact is there is nothing else's that will work,
and that has been true for thousands of years.
It's like the wheel, there is nothing better.
I know tech better than anyone,
& technology.....

.....on a Border is only effective in conjunction
with a Wall. Properly designed and built
Walls work, and the Democrats are lying
when they say they don't. In Israel
the Wall is 99.9% successful.
Will not be any different on our Southern
Border! Hundreds of $Billions saved!

Dec 25, 2018

Merry Christmas!

Dec 25, 2018

I am all alone (poor me) in the White House waiting for the Democrats to come back and make a deal on desperately needed Border Security. At some point the Democrats not wanting to make a deal will cost our Country more money than the Border Wall we are all talking about. Crazy!

Dec 28, 2018

This isn't about the Wall, everybody knows that a Wall will work perfectly (In Israel the Wall works 99.9%). This is only about the Dems not letting Donald Trump & the Republicans have a win. They may have the 10 Senate votes, but we have the issue, Border Security. 2020!

Dec 31, 2018

President and Mrs. Obama built/has a
ten foot Wall around their D.C. mansion/
compound. I agree, totally necessary for their
safety and security. The U.S. needs the same
thing, slightly larger version!

2019

Jan 1, 2019

HAPPY NEW YEAR TO EVERYONE,
INCLUDING THE HATERS AND THE
FAKE NEWS MEDIA! 2019 WILL BE
A FANTASTIC YEAR FOR THOSE
NOT SUFFERING FROM TRUMP
DERANGEMENT SYNDROME.
JUST CALM DOWN AND ENJOY
THE RIDE, GREAT THINGS ARE
HAPPENING FOR OUR COUNTRY!"

Jan 1, 2019

…Remember this. Throughout the ages
some things NEVER get better and
NEVER change. You have Walls
and you have Wheels. It was ALWAYS
that way and it will ALWAYS be that way!
Please explain to the Democrats that there can
NEVER be a replacement for a
good old fashioned WALL!

Jan 1, 2019

Cryin Chuck told his favorite lie when
he used his standard sound bite that
I "slammed the table & walked out of the room.
He had a temper tantrum."
Because I knew he would say that,
and after Nancy said no to proper
Border Security, I politely said bye-bye and left,
no slamming!

Jan 2, 2019

Here we go with Mitt Romney, but so fast!
Question will be, is he a Flake?
I hope not. Would much prefer that Mitt focus
on Border Security and so many other things
where he can be helpful. I won big,
and he didn't. He should be happy for all
Republicans. Be a TEAM player & WIN!

Jan 13, 2019

Democrats should come back to
Washington and work to end the Shutdown,
while at the same time ending the horrible
humanitarian crisis at our Southern Border.
I am in the White House waiting for you!

Jan 14, 2019

The Trump portrait of an unsustainable Border
Crisis is dead on. "In the last two years,
ICE officers made 266,000 arrests of
aliens with Criminal Records,
including those charged or convicted of
100,000 assaults, 30,000 sex crimes &
4000 violent killings." America's Southern....

....Border is eventually going to be
militarized and defended or the
United States, as we have known it, is going
to cease to exist...And Americans will not go
gentle into that good night. Patrick Buchanan.
The great people of our Country demand
proper Border Security NOW!

Jan 14, 2019

Best line in the Elizabeth Warren beer
catastrophe is, to her husband,
"Thank you for being here. I'm glad you're here"
It's their house, he's supposed to be there!

Jan 15, 2019

The Fake News gets crazier and
more dishonest every single day.
Amazing to watch as certain people
covering me, and the tremendous success of this
administration, have truly gone MAD!
Their Fake reporting creates anger and
disunity. Take two weeks off and
come back rested. Chill!

Jan 21, 2019

Nancy Pelosi has behaved so irationally &
has gone so far to the left that she has now
officially become a Radical Democrat.
She is so petrified of the "lefties"
in her party that she has lost control...
And by the way, clean up the streets in
San Francisco, they are disgusting!

Jan 23, 2019

BUILD A WALL & CRIME WILL FALL!
This is the new theme, for two years
until the Wall is finished
(under construction now), of the
Republican Party. Use it and pray!

Jan 27, 2019

Thank you to the Republican National
Committee, (the RNC), who voted
UNANIMOUSLY yesterday to support me in
the upcoming 2020 Election. Considering that
we have done more than any Administration in
the first two years, this should be easy.
More great things now in the works!

Jan 29, 2019

Howard Schultz doesn't have the "guts" to run
for President! Watched him on
@60Minutes last night and I agree with him
that he is not the "smartest person."
Besides, America already has that!
I only hope that Starbucks is still paying me
their rent in Trump Tower!

Jan 29, 2019

In the beautiful Midwest, windchill
temperatures are reaching minus 60 degrees,
the coldest ever recorded. In coming days,
expected to get even colder. People can't last
outside even for minutes. What the hell is
going on with Global Warning?
Please come back fast, we need you!

Feb 1, 2019

No president ever worked harder than me
(cleaning up the mess I inherited)!

Feb 9, 2019

North Korea, under the leadership of
Kim Jong Un, will become a great
Economic Powerhouse. He may surprise some
but he won't surprise me, because I have gotten
to know him & fully understand how capable he
is. North Korea will become a different
kind of Rocket - an Economic one!

Feb 10, 2010

Today Elizabeth Warren, sometimes
referred to by me as Pocahontas, joined the
race for President. Will she run as our
first Native American presidential candidate, or
has she decided that after 32 years,
this is not playing so well anymore?
See you on the campaign TRAIL, Liz!

Feb 20, 2019

Crazy Bernie has just entered the race.
I wish him well!

Feb 22, 2019

I want 5G, and even 6G, technology in the
United States as soon as possible.
It is far more powerful, faster,
and smarter than the current standard.
American companies must step up their efforts,
or get left behind. There is no reason that we
should be lagging behind on.........

Feb 28, 2019

Great meetings and dinner tonight in Vietnam
with Kim Jong Un of North Korea. Very good
dialogue. Resuming tomorrow!

Mar 2, 2019

Oh' I see! Now that the 2 year
Russian Collusion case has fallen apart,
there was no Collusion except bye Crooked
Hillary and the Democrats, they say,
"gee, I have an idea, let's look at
Trump's finances and every deal
he has ever done. Let's follow discredited
Michael Cohen.....

...and the fraudulent and
dishonest statements he made on
Wednesday. No way, it's time to stop this
corrupt and illegally brought Witch Hunt.
Time to start looking at the other side
where real crimes were committed.
Republicans have been abused long enough.
Must end now!

Mar 2, 2019

Wow, just revealed that Michael Cohen
wrote a "love letter to Trump"
manuscript for a new book that he was pushing.
Written and submitted long after
Charlottesville and Helsinki, his phony reasons
for going rogue. Book is exact opposite
of his fake testimony, which now is a lie!

Mar 4, 2019

Presidential Harassment by "crazed"
Democrats at the highest level in
the history of our Country. Likewise,
the most vicious and corrupt
Mainstream Media that any president
has ever had to endure - Yet the most
successful first two years for any

....President. We are WINNING big,
the envy of the WORLD,
but just think what it could be?

Mar 6, 2019

The greatest overreach in the history
of our Country. The Dems are obstructing
justice and will not get anything done.
A big, fat, fishing expedition desperarely in
search of a crime, when in fact the real crime is
what the Dems are doing, and have done!

Mar 12, 2019

At a recent round table meeting of business
executives, & long after formally introducing
Tim Cook of Apple, I quickly referred to
Tim + Apple as Tim/Apple as an easy way to
save time & words. The Fake News was
disparagingly all over this, & it became yet
another bad Trump story!

Mar 12, 2019

Making Daylight Saving Time
permanent is O.K. with me!

Mar 13, 2019

Airplanes are becoming far too complex to fly.
Pilots are no longer needed, but rather
computer scientists from MIT. I see it all the
time in many products. Always seeking
to go one unnecessary step further,
when often old and simpler is far better.
Split second decisions are....

....needed, and the complexity creates danger.
All of this for great cost yet very little gain.
I don't know about you, but I don't want
Albert Einstein to be my pilot.
I want great flying professionals
that are allowed to easily and quickly
take control of a plane!

Mar 15, 2019

VETO!

Mar 16, 2019

.....THIS SHOULD NEVER
HAPPEN TO A PRESIDENT AGAIN!

Mar 17, 2019

Google is helping China and their military,
but not the U.S. Terrible! The good news
is that they helped Crooked Hillary Clinton,
and not Trump....and how did that turn out?

Mar 17, 2019

How is the Paris Environmental Accord
working out for France? After 18 weeks of
rioting by the Yellow Vest Protesters,
I guess not so well! In the meantime,
the United States has gone to the top of
all lists on the Environment.

Mar 19, 2019

Joe Biden got tongue tied over the weekend
when he was unable to properly deliver a
very simple line about his decision to run for
President. Get used to it, another
low I.Q. individual!

Mar 24, 2019

Good Morning, Have A Great Day!

Mar 28, 2019

Very important that OPEC increase the flow of Oil. World Markets are fragile, price of Oil getting too high. Thank you!

Apr 1, 2019

Now that the long awaited Mueller Report
conclusions have been released,
most Democrats and others have gone back to
the pre-Witch Hunt phase of their lives before
Collusion Delusion took over.
Others are pretending that their former hero,
Bob Mueller, no longer exists!

Apr 6, 2019

The press is doing everything within their power to fight the magnificence of the phrase, MAKE AMERICA GREAT AGAIN! They can't stand the fact that this Administration has done more than virtually any other Administration in its first 2yrs. They are truly the ENEMY OF THE PEOPLE!

Apr 7, 2019

Looks like Bob Mueller, team of 13 Trump Haters & Angry Democrats are illegally leaking information to the press while the Fake News Media make up their own stories with or without sources - sources no longer matter to our corrupt & dishonest Mainstream Media, they are a Joke!

Apr 8, 2015

More apprehensions (captures) at the
Southern Border than in many years.
Border Patrol amazing! Country is FULL!
System has been broken for many years.
Democrats in Congress must agree to fix
loopholes - No Open Borders (Crimes & Drugs),
Will Close Southern Border if necessary...

....Mexico must apprehend all illegals and not let
them make the long march up to the
United States, or we will have no other choice
than to Close the Border and/or
institute Tariffs. Our Country is FULL!

Apr 14, 2014

Just out: The USA has the absolute
legal right to have apprehended illegal
immigrants transferred to Sanctuary Cities.
We hereby demand that they be taken care of
at the highest level, especially by the State of
California, which is well known or its poor
management & high taxes!

Apr 15, 2019

What do I know about branding,
maybe nothing (but I did become President!),
but if I were Boeing, I would FIX the Boeing
737 MAX, add some additional great features, &
REBRAND the plane with a new name.
No product has sufered like this one.
But again, what the hell do I know?

Apr 15, 2019

Mueller, and the A.G. based on
Mueller findings (and great intelligence),
have already ruled No Collusion,
No Obstruction. These were crimes
committed by Crooked Hillary, the DNC,
Dirty Cops and others!
INVESTIGATE THE INVESTIGATORS!

Apr 15, 2019

THEY SPIED ON MY CAMPAIGN
(We will never forget)!

Apr 18, 2019

So horrible to watch the massive fire at
Notre Dame Cathedral in Paris.
Perhaps flying water tankers could be used
to put it out. Must act quickly!

Apr 17, 2019

Bernie Sanders and wife should pay the
Pre-Trump Taxes on their almost
$600,000 in income. He is always
complaining about these big TAX CUTS,
except when it benefits him. They made a
fortune off of Trump, but so did everyone else -
and that's a good thing, not a bad thing!

Apr 12, 2019

I believe it will be Crazy Bernie Sanders vs.
Sleepy Joe Biden as the two finalists to run
against maybe the best Economy in the
history of our Country (and MANY other
great things)! I look forward to facing
whoever it may be. May God Rest Their Soul!

Apr 18, 2019

PRESIDENTIAL HARASSMENT!

Apr 23, 2019

In the "old days" if you were President
and you had a good economy, you were
basically immune from criticism. Remember,
"It's the economy stupid." Today I have,
as President, perhaps the greatest economy
in history...and to the Mainstream Media,
it means NOTHING. But it will!

Apr 23, 2019

The Radical Left Democrats, together with their
leaders in the Fake News Media,
have gone totally insane!
I guess that means that the
Republican agenda is working.
Stay tuned for more!

Apr 25, 2019

I didn't call Bob Costa of the
Washington Post, he called me
(Returned his call)! Just more Fake News.

Apr 25, 2019

Welcome to the race Sleepy Joe. I only hope
you have the intelligence, long in doubt,
to wage a successful primary campaign.
It will be nasty - you will be dealing with
people who truly have some very sick &
demented ideas. But if you make it,
I will see you at the Starting Gate!

Apr 26, 2019

Weirdo Tom Steyer, who didn't have the "guts"
or money to run for President, is still trying to
remain relevant by putting himself
on ads begging for impeachment.
He doesn't mention the fact that mine is
perhaps the most successful first 2 year
presidency in history & NO C ORO!

Apr 28, 2019

The Democratic National Committee,
sometimes referred to as the DNC,
is again working its magic in its quest to
destroy Crazy Bernie Sanders....

....for the more traditional, but not
very bright, Sleepy Joe Biden.
Here we go again Bernie, but this time
please show a little more anger and
indignation when you get screwed!

May 10, 2019

Your all time favorite President got
tired of waiting for China to help out and
start buying from our FARMERS,
the greatest anywhere in the World!

May 10, 2019

Looks to me like it's going to be
SleepyCreepy Joe over Crazy Bernie.
Everyone else is fading fast!

May 12, 2019

I won the 2016 Election partially based on no
Tax Returns while I am under audit
(which I still am), and the voters didn't care.
Now the Radical Left Democrats
want to again relitigate this matter.
Make it a part of the 2020 Election!

May 13, 2019

China is DREAMING that Sleepy Joe Biden,
or any of the others, gets elected in 2020.
They LOVE ripping off America!

May 13, 2019

Has anyone noticed that all the Boston
@RedSox have done is WIN since coming
to the White House! Others also have done very
well. The White House visit is becoming the
opposite of being on the cover of
Sports Ilustrated! By the way, the
Boston players were GREAT guys!

May 14, 2019

China will be pumping money into their system
and probably reducing interest rates, as always,
in order to make up for the business they are,
and will be, losing. If the Federal Reserve
ever did a "match," it would be game over,
we win! In any event, China wants a deal!

May 17, 2019

Border Patrol is apprehending record numbers
of people at the Southern Border.
The bad "hombres," of which there are many,
are being detained & will be sent home.
Those which we release under the ridiculous
Catch & Telease loophole,
are being registered and will be removed later!

May 17, 2019

All people that are illegally coming into the
United States now will be removed from our
Country at a later date as we build up our
removal forces and as the laws are changed.
Please do not make yourselves too comfortable,
you will be leaving soon!

May 17, 2019

DRAIN THE SWAMP!

May 17, 2019

MAKE AMERICA GREAT AGAIN!

May 17, 2019

The Fake News Media is hurting our
Country with its fraudulent and highly
inaccurate coverage of Iran.
It is scattershot, poorly sourced (made up),
and DANGEROUS. At least Iran
doesn't know what to think, which at
this point may very well be a good thing!

May 20, 2019

The Mainstream Media has never been as
corrupt and deranged as it is today.
FAKE NEWS is actually the biggest story
of all and is the true ENEMY OF THE
PEOPLE! That's why they refuse to cover the
REAL Russia Hoax. But the American
people are wise to what is going on.....

May 20, 2019

The Failing New York Times (it will pass away
when I leave office in 6 years), and others of
the Fake News Media, keep writing
phony stories about how I didn't use
many banks because they didn't want to do
business with me. WRONG! It is because
I didn't need money. Very old

....fashioned, but true. When you
don't need or want money,
you don't need or want banks.
Banks have always been available to me,
they want to make money.
Fake Media only says this to disparage,
and always uses unnamed sources
(because their sources don't even exist)......

May 23, 2019

Rex Tillerson, a man who is
"dumb as a rock" and totally ill prepared and
ill equipped to be Secretary of State, made up
a story (he got fired) that I was out-prepared
by Vladimir Putin at a meeting in Hamburg,
Germany. I don't think Putin would agree.
Look how the U.S. is doing!

May 26, 2019

North Korea fired off some small weapons,
which disturbed some of my people, and others,
but not me. I have confidence that
Chairman Kim will keep his promise to me,
& also smiled when he called Swampman
Joe Biden a low IQ individual, & worse.
Perhaps that's sending me a signal?

May 29, 2019

I was actually sticking up for Sleepy
Joe Biden while on foreign soil.
Kim Jong Un called him a "low IQ idiot,"
and many other things, whereas I related the
quote of Chairman Kim as a much softer
"low IQ individual." Who could possibly be
upset with that?

Jun 2, 2019

NO COLLUSION, NO OBSTRUCTION, NO NOTHING! "What the Democrats are trying to do is the biggest sin in the impeachment business." David Rivkin, Constitutional Scholar. Meantime, the Dems are getting nothing done in Congress. They are frozen stiff. Get back to work, much to do!

Jun 3, 2019

.@SadiqKhan, who by all accounts has done a
terrible job as Mayor of London,
has been foolishly "nasty" to the visiting
President of the United States, by far the most
important ally of the United Kingdom.
He is a stone cold loser who should focus on
crime in London, not me......

....Kahn reminds me very much of our very
dumb and incompetent Mayor of NYC,
de Blasio, who has also done a terrible
job - only half his height. In any event,
I look forward to being a great friend to the
United Kingdom, and am looking very much
forward to my visit. Landing now!

Jun 3, 2019

Peggy Noonan, the simplistic writer for
Trump Haters all, is stuck in the past glory of
Reagan and has no idea what is happening
with the Radical Left Democrats,
or how vicious and desperate they are.
Mueller had to correct his ridiculous statement,
Peggy never understood it!

Jun 5, 2019

Can you imagine Cryin' Chuck Schumer
saying out loud, for all to hear, that I am
bluffing with respect to putting Tariffs
on Mexico. What a Creep. He would rather
have our Country fail with drugs & Immigration
than give Republicans a win. But he gave
Mexico bad advice, no bluff!

Jun 5, 2019

Plagiarism charge against Sleepy
Joe Biden on his ridiculous Climate Change
Plan is a big problem, but the Corrupt Media
will save him. His other problem is that he is
drawing flies, not people, to his Rallies.
Nobody is showing up, I mean nobody.
You can't win without people!

Jun 6, 2019

A big and beautiful day today!

Jun 8, 2019

For all of the money we are spending,
NASA should NOT be talking about going to
the Moon - We did that 50 years ago.
They should be focused on the much bigger
things we are doing, including Mars (of which
the Moon is a part), Defense and Science!

Jun 13, 2019

I meet and talk to "foreign governments"
every day. I just met with the Queen of England
(U.K.), the Prince of Whales, the P.M. of the
United Kingdom, the P.M. of Ireland,
the President of France and the President of
Poland. We talked about "Everything!"
Should I immediately....

....call the FBI about these calls and meetings?
How ridiculous! I would never be trusted again.
With that being said, my full answer is rarely
played by the Fake News Media.
They purposely leave out the part that matters.

Jun 16, 2019

Happy Father's Day to all,
including my worst and most vicious critics, of
which there are fewer and fewer.
This is a FANTASTIC time to be an American!
KEEP AMERICA GREAT!

Jun 16, 2019

A poll should be done on which is the more
dishonest and deceitful newspaper, the Failing
New York Times or the Amazon (lobbyist)
Washington Post! They are both a disgrace to our
Country, the Enemy of the People,
but I just can't seem to figure out
which is worse? The good.….

.….news is that at the end of 6 years,
after America has been made GREAT
again and I leave the beautiful White House
(do you think the people would demand that
I stay longer? KEEP AMERICA GREAT),
both of these horrible papers will quickly
go out of business & be forever gone!

Jun 18, 2019

The Fake News doesn't report it, but
Republican enthusiasm is at an all time high.
Look what is going on in Orlando, Florida,
right now! People have never seen anything
like it (unless you play a guitar).
Going to be wild - See you later!

Jun 27, 2019

BORING!

Jun 28, 2019

I am in Japan at the G-20, representing our
Country well, but I heard it was not
a good day for Sleepy Joe or Crazy Bernie.
One is exhausted, the other is nuts -
so what's the big deal?

Jun 29, 2019

After some very important meetings, including
my meeting with President Xi of China,
I will be leaving Japan for South Korea
(with President Moon). While there,
if Chairman Kim of North Korea sees this,
I would meet him at the Border/DMZ
just to shake his hand and say Hello(?)!

Jul 3, 2019

We have the greatest economy
anywhere in the world. We have the greatest
military anywhere in the world. Not bad!

Jul 4, 2019

Iran has just issued a New Warning.
Rouhani says that they will Enrich Uranium to
"any amount we want" if there is
no new Nuclear Deal. Be careful with
the threats, Iran. They can come back to
bite you like nobody has been bitten before!

Jul 6, 2019

Joe Biden is a reclamation project.
Some things are just not salvageable.
China and other countries that ripped us off for
years are begging for him.
He deserted our military, our law enforcement
and our healthcare. Added more debt than al
other Presidents combined. Won't win!

Jul 9, 2019

The wacky Ambassador that the U.K. foisted upon the United States is not someone we are thrilled with, a very stupid guy. He should speak to his country, and Prime Minister May, about their failed Brexit negotiation, and not be upset with my criticism of how badly it was...

...handled. I told @theresa_may how to do that deal, but she went her own foolish way-was unable to get it done. A disaster! I don't know the Ambassador but have been told he is a pompous fool. Tell him the USA now has the best Economy & Military anywhere in the World, by far...

....and they are both only getting bigger, better and stronger.....Thank you, Mr. President!

Jul 12, 2019

Will be a big and exciting day at the
White House for Social Media!

Jul 14, 2019

So interesting to see "Progressive"
Democrat Congresswomen,
who originally came from countries whose
governments are a complete and total
catastrophe, the worst, most corrupt and inept
anywhere in the world (if they even have a
functioning government at all), now loudly......

....and viciously telling the people of the
United States, the greatest and most powerful
Nation on earth, how our government
is to be run. Why don't they go back and
help fix the totally broken and crime infested
places from which they came.
Then come back and show us how....

....it is done. These places need your help badly,
you can't leave fast enough. I'm sure that Nancy
Pelosi would be very happy to quickly work out
free travel arrangements!

Jul 16, 2019

The Democrat Congresswomen have been
spewing some of the most vile, hateful,
and disgusting things ever said by a politician
in the House or Senate, & yet they get a
free pass and a big embrace from the
Democrat Party. Horrible anti-Israel,
anti-USA, pro-terrorist & public.....

.....shouting of the F...word, among many
other terrible things, and the petrified Dems
run for the hills. Why isn't the House voting to
rebuke the filthy and hate laced things they have
said? Because they are the Radical Left, and the
Democrats are afraid to take them on. Sad!

Jul 16, 2019

Those Tweets were NOT Racist.
I don't have a Racist bone in my body!
The so-called vote to be taken is a
Democrat con game. Republicans should
not show "weakness" and fall into their trap.
This should be a vote on the filthy language,
statements and lies told by the Democrat......

......Congresswomen, who I truly believe,
based on their actions, hate our Country.
Get a list of the HORRIBLE things they have
said. Omar is polling at 8%, Cortez at 21%.
Nancy Pelosi tried to push them away,
but now they are forever wedded to the
Democrat Party. See you in 2020!

Jul 16, 2019

We will never be a Socialist or Communist Country. IF YOU ARE NOT HAPPY HERE, YOU CAN LEAVE! It is your choice, and your choice alone. This is about love for America. Certain people HATE our Country....

....They are anti-Israel, pro Al-Qaeda, and comment on the 9/11 attack, "some people did something." Radical Left Democrats want Open Borders, which means drugs, crime, human trafficking, and much more....

....Detention facilities are not Concentration Camps! America has never been stronger than it is now — rebuilt Military, highest Stock Market EVER, lowest unemployment and more people working than ever before. Keep America Great!

Jul 19, 2019

It is amazing how the Fake News Media
became "crazed" over the chant
"send her back" by a packed Arena (a record)
crowd in the Great State of North Carolina,
but is totally calm & accepting of the
most vile and disgusting statements
made by the three
Radical Left Congresswomen...

...Mainstream Media, which has lost al
credibility, has either officially or unofficially
become a part of the Radical Left
Democrat Party. It is a sick partnership,
so pathetic to watch! They even covered a tiny
staged crowd as they greeted Foul Mouthed
Omar in Minnesota, a...

....State which I will win in #2020
because they can't stand her and her hatred
of our Country, and they appreciate al that
I have done for them (opening up mining
and MUCH more) which has led to the best
employment & economic year in
Minnesota's long and beautiful history!

Jul 20, 2019

Just spoke to @KanyeWest about
his friend A$AP Rocky's incarceration.
I will be calling the very talented
Prime Minister of Sweden to see what we can
do about helping A$AP Rocky. So many people
would like to see this quickly resolved!

Jul 24, 2019

KEEP AMERICA GREAT!

Jul 24, 2019

When an old Wall at the Southern Border,
that is crumbling and falling over,
built in an important section to keep out
problems, is replaced with a brand new
30 foot high steel and concrete Wall, the Media
says no new Wall has been built. Fake News!
Building lots of Wall!

Jul 25, 2019

TRUTH IS A FORCE OF NATURE!

Jul 26, 2019

Give A$AP Rocky his FREEDOM. We do so
much for Sweden but it doesn't seem to
work the other way around. Sweden should
focus on its real crime problem! #FreeRocky

Jul 29, 2019

Crazy Bernie Sanders recently equated the
City of Baltimore to a THIRD WORLD
COUNTRY! Based on that statement,
I assume that Bernie must now be labeled a
Racist, just as a Republican would if
he used that term and standard! The fact is,
Baltimore can be brought back, maybe......

....even to new heights of success and glory,
but not with King Elijah and that crew.
When the leaders of Baltimore want to see the
City rise again, I am in a very beautiful oval
shaped office waiting for your call!

Aug 2, 2019

Really bad news! The Baltimore house of
Elijah Cummings was robbed. Too bad!

Aug 3, 2019

A$AP Rocky released from prison and
on his way home to the United States from
Sweden. It was a Rocky Week,
get home ASAP A$AP!

Aug 8, 2019

Watching Sleepy Joe Biden making a speech.
Sooo Boring! The LameStream Media
will die in the ratings and clicks with this guy.
It will be over for them, not to mention
the fact that our Country will do poorly with
him. It will be one big crash,
but at least China will be happy!

Aug 13, 2019

Scaramucci, who like so many others
had nothing to do with my Election victory,
is only upset that I didn't want him back in the
Administration (where he desperately wanted
to be). Also, I seldom had time to return his
many calls to me. He just wanted to be on TV!

Aug 14, 2019

Would Chris Cuomo be given a Red Flag for his recent rant? Filthy language and a total loss of control. He shouldn't be alowed to have any weapon. He's nuts!

Aug 15, 2019

I know President Xi of China very well. He is a great leader who very much has the respect of his people. He is also a good man in a "tough business." I have ZERO doubt that if President Xi wants to quickly and humanely solve the Hong Kong problem, he can do it. Personal meeting?

Aug 19, 2019

The New York Times will be out of business soon after I leave office, hopefully in 6 years. They have Zero credibility and are losing a fortune, even now, especially after their massive unfunded liability. I'm fairly certain they'll endorse me just to keep it all going!

Aug 21, 2019

The Fake News LameStream Media is doing everything possible the "create" a U.S. recession, even though the numbers & facts are working totally in the opposite direction. They would be willing to hurt many people, but that doesn't matter to them. Our Economy is sooo strong, sorry!

Aug 21, 2019

Denmark is a very special country with incredible people, but based on Prime Minister Mette Frederiksen's comments, that she would have no interest in discussing the purchase of Greenland, I will be postponing our meeting scheduled in two weeks for another time....

....The Prime Minister was able to save a great deal of expense and effort for both the United States and Denmark by being so direct. I thank her for that and look forward to rescheduling sometime in the future!

Aug 21, 2019

Doing great with China and other Trade Deals.
The only problem we have is Jay Powell and the
Fed. He's like a golfer who can't putt, has no
touch. Big U.S. growth if he does the
right thing, BIG CUT - but don't count
on him! So far he has called it wrong,
and only let us down....

Aug 25, 2019

When I looked up to the sky and jokingly said
"I am the chosen one," at a press conference
two days ago, referring to taking on Trade with
China, little did I realize that the media would
claim that I had a "Messiah complex." They
knew I was kidding, being sarcastic, and just....

....having fun. I was smiling as I looked up and
around. The MANY reporters with me were
smiling also. They knew the TRUTH...
And yet when I saw the reporting,
CNN, MSNBC and other Fake News outlets
covered it as serious news & me thinking of
myself as the Messiah. No more trust!

Aug 28, 2019

Can you believe it? I'm at 94% approval in
the Republican Party, and have Three Stooges
running against me. One is
"Mr. Appalachian Trail" who was actually in
Argentina for bad reasons....

....Another is a one-time BAD Congressman
from Ilinois who lost in his second term by a
landslide, then failed in radio. The third is
a man who couldn't stand up
straight while receiving an award.
I should be able to take them!

Sep 3, 2019

For all of the "geniuses" out there, many who
have been in other administrations and
"taken to the cleaners" by China, that want me to
get together with the EU and others to go after
China Trade practices remember,
the EU & al treat us VERY unfairly on
Trade also. Will change!

Sep 4, 2019

The incompetent Mayor of London,
Sadiq Khan, was bothered that
I played a very fast round of golf yesterday.
Many Pols exercise for hours, or travel for weeks.
Me, I run through one of my courses
(very inexpensive). President Obama would
fly to Hawaii. Kahn should focus on....

...."knife crime," which is totally out of
control in London. People are afraid to
even walk the streets. He is a terrible mayor
who should stay out of our business!

Sep 8, 2019

The Failing New York Times stated, in an article written by Obama flunky Peter Baker (who lovingly wrote Obama book),"Even after the President forecast the storm to include Alabama." THIS IS NOT TRUE. I said, VERY EARLY ON, that it MAY EVEN hit Alabama. A BIG DIFFERENCE.....

...FAKE NE WS. I would like very much to stop referring to this ridiculous story, but the LameStream Media just won't let it alone. They always have to have the last word, even though they know they are defrauding & deceiving the public. The public knows that the Media is corrupt!

Sep 9, 2019

I know nothing about an Air Force
plane landing at an airport (which I do not own
and have nothing to do with) near Turnberry
Resort (which I do own) in Scotland,
and filing up with fuel, with the crew staying
overnight at Turnberry (they have good taste!).
NOTHING TO DO WITH ME

The Federal Reserve should get our interest rates down to ZERO, or less, and we should then start to refinance our debt. INTEREST COST COULD BE BROUGHT WAY DOWN, while at the same time substantially lengthening the term. We have the great currency, power, and balance sheet.....

....The USA should always be paying the the lowest rate. No Inflation! It is only the naïveté of Jay Powell and the Federal Reserve that doesn't alow us to do what other countries are already doing. A once in a lifetime opportunity that we are missing because of "Boneheads."

"A Very Stable Genius!" Thank you.

Sep 14, 2019

Who the hell is Joy-Ann Reid? Never met her,
she knows ZERO about me, has NO talent, and
truly doesn't have the "it" factor needed
for success in showbiz. Had a bad reputation,
and now works for the Comcast/NBC losers
making up phony stories about me.
Low Ratings. Fake News!

Sep 15, 2019

Now the Radical Left Democrats
and their Partner, the LameStream Media, are
after Brett Kavanaugh again, talking loudly of
their favorite word, impeachment.
He is an innocent man who has been treated
HORRIBLY. Such lies about him.
They want to scare him into turning Liberal!

Sep 16, 2019

PLENTY OF OIL!

They failed on the Mueller Report,
they failed on Robert Mueller's testimony,
they failed on everything else, so now the
Democrats are trying to build a case that
I enrich myself by being President.
Good idea, except I will, and have always
expected to, lose BILLIONS of DOLLARS..

....for the privilege of being your President -
and doing the best job that has been done in
many decades. I am far beyond somebody
paying for a hotel room for the evening, or filing
up a gas tank at an airport I do not own.
These Radical Left Democrats are CRAZY!
Obama Netflix?

Sep 22, 2019

Some of the best Economic Numbers our Country has ever experienced are happening right now. This is despite a Crooked and Demented Deep State, and a probably ilegal Democrat/Fake News Media Partnership the likes of which the world has never seen. MAKE AMERICA GREAT AGAIN!

Sep 25, 2019

PRESIDENTIAL HARASSMENT!

Sep 25, 2019

There has been no President in the history of our Country who has been treated so badly as I have. The Democrats are frozen with hatred and fear. They get nothing done. This should never be alowed to happen to another President. Witch Hunt!

Sep 25, 2019

Will the Democrats apologize after
seeing what was said on the call with the
Ukrainian President? They should,
a perfect call - got them by surprise!

Sep 26, 2019

THE GREATEST SCAM IN THE
HISTORY OF AMERICAN POLITICS!

Sep 27, 2019

Iran wanted me to lift the sanctions
imposed on them in order to meet.
I said, of course, NO!

Sep 28, 2019

If that perfect phone call with the President of
Ukraine Isn't considered appropriate,
then no future President can EVER
again speak to another foreign leader!

Sep 28, 2019

PRESIDENTIAL HARASSMENT!

Sep 28, 2019

MAKE AMERICA GREAT AGAIN!

Sep 28, 2019

KEEP AMERICA GREAT!

Oct 2, 2019

As I learn more and more each day,
I am coming to the conclusion that
what is taking place is not an impeachment,
it is a COUP, intended to take away
the Power of the....

....People, their VOTE, their Freedoms,
their Second Amendment, Religion,
Military, Border Wall, and their
God-given rights as a Citizen of
The United States of America!

Oct 3, 2019

All the Do Nothing Democrats are focused
on is Impeaching the President for having
a very good conversation with the Ukrainian
President. I knew that many people were
listening, even have a transcript.
They have been at this "stuff" from the day
I got elected. Bad for Country!

Oct 3, 2019

#DONOTHINGDEMS

Oct 3, 2019

The Do Nothing Democrats should be
focused on building up our Country,
not wasting everyone's time and energy on
BULLSHIT, which is what they have
been doing ever since I got overwhelmingly
elected in 2016, 223-306. Get a better
candidate this time, you'll need it!

Oct 4, 2019

ELECTION INTERFERENCE!

Oct 5, 2019

"Adam Schiff's connection to the Whistleblower is coming to light." @FoxNews These facts, and others, make it impossible for the ridiculous impeachment "scam" to go forward! Schiff has also committed a crime, perhaps treason, in making up a horrible statement and reading....

....it to Congress, and the American people, as though it was the statement of the President of the United States, me. He did it to fool Congress and the public in order to make me look BAD. He is a sick puppy!

Oct 5, 2019

The Media is "Fixed" and Corrupt. It bears no
relationship to the truth.
The @nytimes & @washingtonpost
are pure fiction. Totally dishonest reporting!

Oct 5, 2019

The so-called Whistleblower's account of my
perfect phone call is "way off," not even close.
Schiff and Pelosi never thought I would release
the transcript of the call. Got them by surprise,
they got caught. This is a fraud against the
American people!

Oct 6, 2019

Somebody please wake up Mitt Romney
and tell him that my conversation with the
Ukrainian President was a congenial and very
appropriate one, and my statement on China
pertained to corruption, not politics.
If Mitt worked this hard on Obama,
he could have won. Sadly, he choked!

Oct 6, 2019

Mitt Romney never knew how to win.
He is a pompous "ass" who has been
fighting me from the beginning,
except when he begged me for my
endorsement for his Senate run
(I gave it to him), and when he begged me
to be Secretary of State
(I didn't give it to him).
He is so bad for R's!

Oct 6, 2019

I'm hearing that the Great People of
Utah are considering their vote for their
Pompous Senator, Mitt Romney, to be a big
mistake. I agree! He is a fool who is
playing right into the hands of the
Do Nothing Democrats!
#IMPEACHMITTROMNEY

Oct 6, 2019

So Crooked Hillary Clinton can delete
and acid wash 33,000 emails AFTER getting a
Subpoena from the United States Congress,
but I can't make one totally appropriate
telephone call to the President of Ukraine?
Witch Hunt!

Oct 7, 2019

The Democrats are lucky that they don't have
any Mitt Romney types. They may be lousy
politicians, with really bad policies
(Open Borders, Sanctuary Cities etc.),
but they stick together!

The Biden family was PAID OFF, pure and simple! The fake news must stop making excuses for something that is totally inexcusable. Sleepy Joe said he never spoke to the Ukrainian company, and then the picture came out where he was playing golf with the company boss and Hunter.....

....And by the way, I would LOVE running against 1% Joe Biden - I just don't think it's going to happen. Sleepy Joe won't get to the starting gate, & based on al of the money he & his family probably "extorted," Joe should hang it up. I wouldn't want him dealing with China & U!

DRAIN THE SWAMP!

Oct 7, 2019

Sleepy Eyes Chuck Todd of "Meet the Press" had a total meltdown in his interview with highly reaspected Senator @RonJohnsonWl. Seems that a not very bright Chuck just wasn't getting the answers he was looking for in order to make me look as bad as possible. I did NOTHING wrong!

Oct 7, 2019

Unemployment Rate just dropped to 3.5%, the lowest in more that 50 years. Is that an impeachable event for your President?

Oct 8, 2019

I was elected on getting out of these
ridiculous endless wars, where our
great Military functions as a policing
operation to the benefit of people who don't
even like the USA. The two most unhappy
countries at this move are Russia & China,
because they love seeing us bogged…..

….down, watching over a quagmire,
& spending big dollars to do so. When I took
over, our Military was totally depleted. Now
it is stronger than ever before. The endless
and ridiculous wars are ENDING! We will be
focused on the big picture, knowing we can
always go back & BLAST!

Oct 8, 2019

As I have stated strongly before, and just to
reiterate, if Turkey does anything that I,
in my great and unmatched wisdom,
consider to be off limits, I will totally
destroy and obliterate the Economy of Turkey
(I've done before!). They must,
with Europe and others, watch over...

....the captured ISIS fighters and families.
The U.S. has done far more than anyone could
have ever expected, including the capture of
100% of the ISIS Caliphate. It is time now for
others in the region, some of great wealth, to
protect their own territory.
THE USA IS GREAT!

Oct 9, 2019

....No Pressure at all said Ukraine! Very
congenial, a perfect call. The Whistleblower and
others spoke BEFORE seeing the Transcript.
Now they must apologize to me and
stop this ridiculous impeachment!

Oct 10, 2019

Only 25 percent want the President Impeached,
which is pretty low considering the
volume of Fake News coverage, but pretty
high considering the fact that I did
NOTHING wrong. It is all just a
continuation of the greatest Scam and
Witch Hunt in the history of our Country!

Oct 12, 2019

WHERE'S HUNTER?

Oct 13, 2019

The deal I just made with China is, by far,
the greatest and biggest deal ever made
for our Great Patriot Farmers in the history
of our Country. In fact, there is a question as
to whether or not this much product can be
produced? Our farmers will figure it out.
Thank you China!

Oct 13, 2019

So now they are after the legendary
"crime buster" and greatest Mayor in the
history of NYC, Rudy Giuliani.
He may seem a little rough around the edges
sometimes, but he is also a great guy and
wonderful lawyer. Such a one sided Witch
Hunt going on in USA. Deep State. Shameful!

Oct 14, 2019

Vote for good guy @seanspicer tonight on
Dancing With The Stars.
He has always been there for us!

Oct 15, 2019

After defeating 100% of the ISIS Caliphate,
I largely moved our troops out of Syria.
Let Syria and Assad protect the
Kurds and fight Turkey for their own land.
I said to my Generals, why should
we be fighting for Syria....

....and Assad to protect the land of our enemy?
Anyone who wants to assist Syria in
protecting the Kurds is good with me,
whether it is Russia, China, or Napoleon
Bonaparte. I hope they all do great,
we are 7,000 miles away!

Oct 15, 2019

Shifty Schiff now seems to think they
don't need the Whistleblower,
who started the whole Scam.
The reason is that the Whistleblower has
lost all credibility because the story is so
far from the facts on the Transcript. Also,
the second Whistleblower is
no longer even mentioned!

Oct 16, 2019

Shifty Adam Schiff wants to rest
his entire case on a Whistleblower
who he now says can't testify, & the reason he
can't testify is that he is afraid to do so because
his account of the Presidential telephone call
is a fraud & totally different from the
actual transcribed call...

.... It also brings Shifty's fraudulent
MADE UP CALL, which he read to the
United States Congress pretending it to
be the words of President Trump,
which they were not! Nancy Pelosi is
involved in this fraud in that she
confirmed his fraudulent words on
@GMA, and much more!

Oct 16, 2019

Just out: MEDIAN HOUSEHOLD INCOME
IS AT THE HIGHEST POINT EVER,
EVER, EVER! How about saying it this way,
IN THE HISTORY OF OUR COUNTRY!
Also, MORE PEOPLE WORKING TODAY
IN THE USA THAN AT ANY TIME IN
HISTORY! Tough numbers for the
Radical Left Democrats to beat!
Impeach the Pres.

Oct 17, 2019

Nancy Pelosi needs help fast! There is either
something wrong with her "upstairs,"
or she just plain doesn't like our great Country.
She had a total meltdown in the
White House today. It was very sad to watch.
Pray for her, she is a very sick person!

Oct 20, 2019

Such a disgrace that the Do Nothing
Democrats are doing just as their name
suggests, Doing Nothing! USMCA anyone?

Oct 20, 2019

So now Crooked Hillary is at it again!
She is calling Congresswoman Tulsi Gabbard
"a Russian favorite," and Jill Stein
"a Russian asset." As you may have heard,
I was called a big Russia lover also
(actually, I do like Russian people. I like all
people!). Hillary's gone Crazy!

Oct 23, 2019

Can't believe that Nervous Nancy Pelosi
isn't moving faster on USMCA.
Her people want it, they don't know why
she isn't putting it up for a bipartisan vote.
Taking too long!

Oct 24, 2019

It would be really great if the people within the
Trump Administration, all well-meaning and
good (I hope!), could stop hiring
Never Trumpers, who are worse than the
Do Nothing Democrats. Nothing good
will ever come from them!

Oct 26, 2019

To Tim: The Button on the IPhone was
FAR better than the Swipe!

Oct 26, 2019

....

Oct 27, 2019

Something very big has just happened!

Oct 28, 2019

We have declassified a picture of the
wonderful dog (name not declassified)
that did such a GREAT JOB in capturing
and killing the Leader of ISIS,
Abu Bakr al-Baghdadi!

Nov 2, 2019

ISIS has a new leader.
We know exactly who he is!

Nov 2, 2019

Oh no, Beto just dropped out of race for
President despite him saying he was
"born for this." I don't think so!

Nov 5, 2019

Many people say they know me, claiming to be
"best friends" and really close etc.,
when I don't know these people at al.
This happens, I suppose, to all who become
President. With that being stated,
I don't know, to the best of my knowledge,
a man named Michael Esposito.....

....I don't like him using my name to build his
consulting company, or whatever.
Please advise his clients and
Administration officials accordingly.

Nov 7, 2019

Stock Markets (all three) hit another
ALL TIME & HISTORIC HIGH yesterday!
You are sooo lucky to have me as
your President (just kidding!).
Spend your money well!

PRESIDENTIAL HARASSMENT!

I recommend that Nervous Nancy Pelosi
(who backed up Schiff's lie), Shifty
Adam Schiff, Sleepy Joe Biden,
the Whistleblower (who miraculously
disappeared after I released the transcript of
the call), the 2nd Whistleblower (who also
disappeared), & the I.G., be part of the list!

....Whatever happened to the
so-called "informer" to Whistleblower #1?
Seems to have disappeared after I released
the Transcript of the call. Shouldn't he be
on the list to testify? Witch Hunt!

Nov 12, 2019

In order to continue being the most
Transparent President in history,
I will be releasing sometime this week
the Transcript of the first, and therefore
most important, phone call I had with the
President of Ukraine. I am sure you
will find it tantalizing!

Nov 14, 2019

NEVER TRUMPERS!

Nov 14, 2019

READ THE TRANSCRIPT!

Nov 14, 2019

Wow! Was just told that my son's book,
"Triggered," is Number One on
The New York Times Bestseller List.
Congratulations Don!

Nov 16, 2019

So they now convict Roger Stone of lying and
want to jail him for many years to come.
Well, what about Crooked Hillary, Comey,
Strzok, Page, McCabe, Brennan, Clapper,
Shifty Schiff, Ohr & Nellie, Steele &
al of the others, including even
Mueller himself? Didn't they lie?....

...A double standard like never seen before
in the history of our Country?

Nov 19, 2019

Our Crazy, Do Nothing (where's USMCA, infrastructure, lower drug pricing & much more?) Speaker of the House, Nervous Nancy Pelosi, who is petrified by her Radical Left knowing she will soon be gone (they & Fake News Media are her BOSS), suggested on Sunday's DEFACE THE NATION....

....that I testify about the phony Impeachment Witch Hunt. She also said I could do it in writing. Even though I did nothing wrong, and don't like giving credibility to this No Due Process Hoax, I like the idea & will, in order to get Congress focused again, strongly consider it!

Nov 19, 2019

Nancy Pelosi just stated that "it is dangerous to
let the voters decide Trump's fate."
@FoxNews In other words, she thinks
I'm going to win and doesn't want to take a
chance on letting the voters decide.
Like Al Green, she wants to change our
voting system. Wow, she's CRAZY!

Nov 21, 2019

During my visit yesterday to Austin,
Texas, for the startup of the new Mac Pro,
& the discussion of a new one $billion campus,
also in Texas, I asked Tim Cook to see if he
could get Apple involved in building 5G
in the U.S. They have it all - Money,
Technology, Vision & Cook!l

Nov 21, 2019

If this were a prizefight, they'd stop it!

Dec 3, 2019

The Do Nothing Democrats get 3
Constitutional lawyers for their
Impeachment hoax (they will need them!),
the Republicans get one. Oh, that sounds fair!

Dec 3, 2019

Thank you to Great Republican
@SenJohnKennedy for the job he did in
representing both the Republican Party and
myself against Sleepy Eyes Chuck Todd
on Meet the Depressed!

Dec 3, 2019

Mini Mike Bloomberg has instructed his
third rate news organization not to
investigate him or any Democrat, but to
go after President Trump, only. The Failing
New York Times thinks that is O.K.,
because their hatred & bias is so great
they can't even see straight. It's not O.K.!

Dec 5, 2019

When I said, in my phone call to the
President of Ukraine, "I would like you
to do US a favor though because our
country has been through a lot and
Ukraine knows a lot about it." With the word
"us" I am referring to the United States, our
Country. I then went on to say that……

….."I would like to have the Attorney
General (of the United States) call you or
your people….." This, based on what
I have seen, is their big point –
and it is no point at a all (except for a
big win for me!). The Democrats should
apologize to the American people!

Dec 6, 2019

Nancy Pelosi just had a nervous fit.
She hates that we will soon have
182 great new judges and s000 much more.
Stock Market and employment records.
She says she "prays for the President."
I don't believe her, not even close. Help the
homeless in your district Nancy. USMCA?

Dec 6, 2019

The story today that we are sending
12,000 troops to Saudi Arabia is false or,
to put it more accurately, Fake News!

Dec 7, 2019

Why is the World Bank loaning money
to China? Can this be possible?
China has plenty of money, and if they don't,
they create it. STOP!

Dec 8, 2019

Our Economy is the envy of the World!

Dec 13, 2019

Getting VERY close to a BIG DEAL with
China. They want it, and so do we!

Dec 13, 2019

Congratulations to Boris Johnson on his great
WIN! Britain and the United States will now be
free to strike a massive new Trade Deal after
BREXIT. This deal has the potential to be far
bigger and more lucrative than any deal that
could be made with the E.U. Celebrate Boris!

Dec 14, 2019

How do you get Impeached when you
have done NOTHING wrong (a perfect call),
have created the best economy in the history
of our Country, rebuilt our Military,
fixed the V.A. (Choice!), cut Taxes & Regs,
protected your 2nd A, created Jobs, Jobs, Jobs,
and soooo much more? Crazy!

Dec 14, 2019

It's not fair that I'm being Impeached
when I've done absolutely nothing wrong!
The Radical Left, Do Nothing Democrats
have become the Party of Hate.
They are so bad for our Country!

Dec 15, 2019

Chuck Schumer sat for years during the
Obama Administration and watched as China
ripped off the United States. He & the
Do Nothing Democrats did NOTHING
as this $ carnage took place. Now,
without even seeing it, he snipes at our
GREAT new deal with China.
Too bad Cryin' Chuck!

Dec 17, 2019

New Stock Market high! I will never
get bored of telling you that -
and we will never get tired of winning!

Dec 18, 2019

Good marks and reviews on the letter
I sent to Pelosi today. She is the worst!
No wonder with people like her and
Cryin' Chuck Schumer, D.C. has been such a
mess for so long - and that includes the
previous administration who (and now we
know for sure) SPIED on my campaign.

Dec 18, 2019

Can you believe that I will be impeached today
by the Radical Left, Do Nothing Democrats,
AND I DID NOTHING WRONG!
A terrible Thing. Read the Transcripts.
This should never happen to another
President again. Say a PRAYER!

Dec 19, 2019

SUCH ATROCIOUS LIES BY
THE RADICAL LEFT, DO NOTHING
DEMOCRATS. THIS IS AN ASSAULT ON
AMERICA, AND AN ASSAULT ON THE
REPUBLICAN PARTY!!!!

Dec 19, 2019

100% Republican Vote. That's what
people are talking about. The Republicans are
united like never before!

Dec 20, 2019

PRESIDENTIAL HARASSMENT!

Dec 20, 2019

So after the Democrats gave me no Due Process
in the House, no lawyers, no witnesses,
no nothing, they now want to tell the Senate
how to run their trial. Actually, they have
zero proof of anything, they will never
even show up. They want out.
I want an immediate trial!

Dec 21, 2019

I guess the magazine, "Christianity Today,"
is looking for Elizabeth Warren,
Bernie Sanders, or those of the socialist/
communist bent, to guard their religion.
How about Sleepy Joe? The fact is,
no President has ever done what I have done
for Evangelicals, or religion itself!

Dec 21, 2019

Nancy Pelosi is looking for a
Quid Pro Quo with the Senate.
Why aren't we Impeaching her?

Dec 23, 2019

The Democrats and Crooked Hillary
paid for & provided a Fake Dossier,
with phony information gotten from foreign
sources, pushed it to the corrupt media &
Dirty Cops, & have now been caught.
They spied on my campaign, then tried to
cover it up - Just Like Watergate, but bigger!

Dec 24, 2019

Pelosi gives us the most unfair trial in the
history of the U.S. Congress, and now she is
crying for fairness in the Senate,
and breaking all rules while doing so. She lost
Congress once, she will do it again!

Dec 25, 2019

MERRY CHRISTMAS!

Dec 26, 2019

The Radical Left, Do Nothing Democrats
said they wanted to RUSH everything
through to the Senate because
"President Trump is a threat to National
Security" (they are vicious, will say anything!),
but now they don't want to go fast anymore,
they want to go very slowly. Liars!

Dec 29, 2019

California and New York must do something
about their TREMENDOUS
Homeless problems. They are setting records!
If their Governors can't handle the situation,
which they should be able to do very easily, they
must call and "politely" ask for help.
Would be so easy with competence!

Dec 29, 2019

So sad to see that New York City and State are
falling apart. All they want to do is investigate
to make me hate them even more than I should.
Governor Cuomo has lost control, and lost his
mind. Very bad for the homeless and all!

2020

Jan 1, 2020

HAPPY NEW YEAR!

Jan 3, 2020

Iran never won a war,
but never lost a negotiation!

Jan 4, 2020

General Qassem Soleimani has killed or
badly wounded thousands of Americans
over an extended period of time, and was
plotting to kill many more ... but got caught!
He was directly and indirectly responsible
for the death of millions of people,
including the recent large number....

....of PROTESTERS killed in Iran itself.
While Iran will never be able to
properly admit it, Soleimani was both hated
and feared within the country. They are not
nearly as saddened as the leaders will let the
outside world believe. He should have been
taken out many years ago!

Jan 5, 2020

As hard as I work, & as successful as our
Country has become with our Economy,
our Military & everything else, it is ashame
that the Democrats make us spend
so much time & money on this ridiculous
Impeachment Lite Hoax. I should be able to
devote all of my time to the REAL USA!

Jan 5, 2020

The United States just spent
Two Trillion Dollars on Military Equipment.
We are the biggest and by far the BEST
in the World! If Iran attacks an American Base,
or any American, we will be sending some of
that brand new beautiful equipment their way...
and without hesitation!

Jan 6, 2020

These Media Posts will serve as
notification to the United States Congress that
should Iran strike any U.S. person or target,
the United States will quickly &
fully strike back, & perhaps in a
disproportionate manner. Such legal notice
is not required, but is given nevertheless!

Jan 7, 2020

IRAN WILL NEVER HAVE
A NUCLEAR WEAPON!

Jan 8, 2020

All is well! Missiles launched from Iran
at two military bases located in Iraq.
Assessment of casualties & damages taking place
now. So far, so good! We have the
most powerful and well equipped military
anywhere in the world, by far! I will be
making a statement tomorrow morning.

Jan 9, 2020

Pelosi doesn't want to hand over
The Articles of Impeachment,
which were fraudulently produced
by corrupt politicians like Shifty Schiff in the
first place, because after all of these years of
investigations and persecution, they show
no crimes and are a joke and a scam!

Jan 10, 2020

U.S. Cancer Death Rate Lowest
In Recorded History! A lot of good news
coming out of this Administration.

Jan 12, 2020

Nancy Pelosi will go down as
the absolute worst Speaker of the
House in U.S. history!

Jan 12, 2020

95% Approval Rating in the Republican Party,
a record. 53% Approval Rating overall
(can we add 7 to 10 percent because of the
Trump "thing?"). Thank you!

Jan 13, 2020

To the leaders of Iran - DO NOT KILL
YOUR PROTESTERS. Thousands have
already been killed or imprisoned by you, and the
World is watching. More importantly,
the USA is watching. Turn your internet
back on and let reporters roam free! Stop the
killing of your great Iranian people!

Jan 13, 2020

Wow! Crazy Bernie Sanders is surging
in the polls, looking very good against his
opponents in the Do Nothing Party. So what
does this all mean? Stay tuned!

Jan 14, 2020

Really Big Breaking News (Kidding):
Booker, who was in zero polling territory, just
dropped out of the Democrat Presidential
Primary Race. Now I can rest easy tonight.
I was sooo concerned that I wuld someday
have to go head to head with him!

Jan 15, 2020

Cryin' Chuck Schumer just said,
"The American people want a fair trial in the
Senate." True, but why didn't Nervous Nancy
and Corrupt politician Adam "Shifty"
Schiff give us a fair trial in the House.
It was the most lopsided & unfair basement
hearing in the history of Congress!

Jan 17, 2020

I JUST GOT IMPEACHED FOR
MAKING A PERFECT PHONE CALL!

Jan 18, 2020

The so-called "Supreme Leader" of Iran,
who has not been so Supreme lately,
had some nasty things to say about the
United States and Europe. Their economy is
crashing, and their people are suffering.
He should be very careful with his words!

Jan 19, 2020

A massive 200 Billion Dollar Sea Wall,
built around New York to protect it from
rare storms, is a costly, foolish &
environmentally unfriendly idea that, when
needed, probably won't work anyway. It will also
look terrible. Sorry, you'll just have to get
your mops & buckets ready!

Jan 19, 2020

....BUT THE BEST IS YET TO COME!

Jan 21, 2020

USA! USA! USA!

Jan 21, 2020

It was exactly three years ago today,
January 20, 2017, that I was sworn into office.
So appropriate that today is also MLK jr DAY.
African-American Unemployment
is the LOWEST in the history of our Country,
by far. Also, best Poverty, Youth,
and Employment numbers, ever. Great!

Jan 21, 2020

I will NEVER allow our great Second
Amendment to go unprotected,
not even a little bit!

Jan 21, 2020

Heading to Davos, Switzerland,
to meet with World and Business Leaders
and bring Good Policy and additional
Hundreds of Billions of Dollars back to the
United States of America!
We are now NUMBER ONE
in the Universe, by FAR!!

Jan 23, 2020

They are taking the nomination away from
Bernie for a second time. Rigged!

Jan 25, 2020

China has been working very hard
to contain the Coronavirus.
The United States greatly appreciates
their efforts and transparency.
It will all work out well. In particular, on behalf
of the American People,
I want to thank President Xi!

Jan 27, 2020

Reports are that basketball great
Kobe Bryant and three others have been
killed in a helicopter crash in California.
That is terrible news!

Jan 28, 2020

READ THE TRANSCRIPTS!

Jan 29, 2020

Are you better off now than you were
three years ago? Almost everyone say YES!

Jan 29, 2020

Heading to New Jersey. Big Rally,
in fact, Really Big Rally!

Jan 31, 2020

Working closely with China and
others on Coronavirus outbreak.
Only 5 people in U.S., all in good recovery.

Feb 4, 2020

Where's the Whistleblower?
Where's the second Whistleblower?
Where's the Informer? Why did Corrupt
politician Schiff MAKE UP my conversation
with the Ukrainian President???
Why didn't the House do its job?
And sooo much more!

Feb 9, 2020

Pete Rose played Major League Baseball
for 24 seasons, from 1963-1986,
and had more hits, 4,256, than any
other player (by a wide margin). He gambled, but
only on his own team winning,
and paid a decades long price.
GET PETE ROSE INTO THE
BASEBALL HALL OF FAME.
It's Time!

Feb 9, 2020

Thank you to everyone for all of the
great reviews I have gotten on my
State of the Union Speech. It was an immense
honor for me to have presented it to you
and the citizens of our very strong
and wonderful Country!

Feb 10, 2020

MAKE AMERICA GREAT AGAIN
and then, KEEP AMERICA GREAT!

Feb 12, 2020

Elizabeth Warren, sometimes referred to as
Pocahontas, is having a really bad night.
I think she is sending signals that
she wants out. Calling for unity is her way of
getting there, going home, and having a
"nice cold beer" with her husband!

Feb 12, 2020

Bootedgeedge (Buttigieg) is doing pretty well
tonight. Giving Crazy Bernie a run
for his money. Very interesting!

Feb 14, 2020

Mini Mike is a 5'4" mass of dead energy who
does not want to be on the debate stage
with these professional politicians. No boxes
please. He hates Crazy Bernie and will,
with enough money, possibly stop him.
Bernie's people will go nuts!

Feb 15, 2020

Great honor, I think? Mark Zuckerberg
recently stated that "Donald J. Trump is
Number 1 on Facebook. Number 2 is
Prime Minister Modi of India:' Actually,
I am going to India in two weeks.
Looking forward to it!

Feb 18, 2020

HAPPY PRESIDENT'S DAY!

Feb 19, 2020

Mini Mike. No, I would rather run against you!

Feb 22, 2020

IF OUR FORMALLY TARGETED
FARMERS NEED ADDITIONAL AID
UNTIL SUCH TIME AS THE TRADE
DEALS WITH CHINA, MEXICO,
CANADA AND OTHERS
FULLY KICK IN, THAT AID WILL
BE PROVIDED BY THE FEDERAL
GOVERNMENT, PAID FOR OUT OF
THE MASSIVE TARIFF MONEY
COMING INTO THE USA!

Feb 24, 2020

Somebody please tell incompetent
(thanks for my high poll numbers) & corrupt
politician Adam "Shifty" Schiff to stop leaking
Classified information or, even worse,
made up information, to the Fake News Media.
Someday he will be caught, & that will be
a very unpleasant experience!

Feb 28, 2020

So, the Coronavirus, which started
in China and spread to various countries
throughout the world, but very slowly in the
U.S. because President Trump closed
our border, and ended flights, VERY EARLY,
is now being blamed, by the Do Nothing
Democrats, to be the fault of "Trump'.

Mar 3, 2020

They are staging a coup against Bernie!

Mar 4, 2020

The biggest loser tonight, by far, is
Mini Mike Bloomberg. His "political"
consultants took him for a ride.
$700 million washed down the drain,
and he got nothing for it but the nickname
Mini Mike, and the complete destruction
of his reputation. Way to go Mike!

Mar 4, 2020

Elizabeth "Pocahontas" Warren, other than
Mini Mike, was the loser of the night.
She didn't even come close to winning
her home state of Massachusetts.
Well, now she can just sit back with
her husband and have a nice cold beer!

Mar 4, 2020

MAKE AMERICA GREAT AGAIN
and then, KEEP AMERICA GREAT!!!!

Mar 5, 2020

Wow! If Elizabeth Warren wasn't in the race,
Bernie Sanders would have EASILY won
Massachusetts, Minnesota and Texas,
not to mention various other states.
Our modern day Pocahontas won't go down in
history as a winner, but she may very well go
down as the all time great SPOILER!

Mar 9, 2020

The Fake News Media and their partner,
the Democrat Party, is doing everything
within its semi-considerable power
(it used to be greater!) to inflame the
CoronaVirus situation, far beyond
what the facts would warrant. Surgeon General,
"The risk is low to the average American."

Mar 10, 2020

So much FAKE NEWS!

Mar 10, 2020

So last year 37,000 Americans died from
the common Flu. It averages between 27,000
and 70,000 per year. Nothing is shut down,
life & the economy go on. At this moment
there are 546 confirmed cases of CoronaVirus,
with 22 deaths. Think about that!

Mar 12, 2020

The Media should view this as a time of unity
and strength. We have a common enemy,
actually, an enemy of the World,
the CoronaVirus. We must beat it as quickly and
safely as possible. There is nothing
more important to me than the life & safety
of the United States!

Mar 14, 2020

I will be having a news conference
today at 3:00 P.M., The White House.
Topic: CoronaVirus!

Mar 15, 2020

SOCIAL DISTANCING!

Mar 16, 2020

We are doing very precise Medical Screenings
at our airports. Pardon the interruptions
and delays, we are moving as quickly
as possible, but it is very important
that we be vigilant and careful.
We must get it right. Safety first!

Mar 16, 2020

God Bless the USA!

Mar 17, 2020

Everybody is so well unified and
working so hard. It is a beautiful thing to see.
They love our great Country. We will end up
being stronger than ever before!

Mar 17, 2020

The United States will be powerfully
supporting those industries, like Airlines
and others, that are particularly affected
by the Chinese Virus. We will be stronger
than ever before!

Mar 18, 2020

The world is at war with a hidden enemy.
WE WILL WIN!

Mar 18, 2020

For the people that are now out of
work because of the important and
necessary containment policies,
for instance the shutting down of hotels,
bars and restaurants, money will soon
be coming to you. The onslaught of the
Chinese Virus is not your fault!
Will be stronger than ever!

Mar 22, 2020

HYDROXYCHLOROQUINE & AZITHROMYCIN, taken together, have a real chance to be one of the biggest game changers in the history of medicine. The FDA has moved mountains - Thank You! Hopefully they will BOTH (H works better with A, International Journal of Antimicrobial Agents).....

....be put in use IMMEDIATELY. PEOPLE ARE DYING, MOVE FAST, and GOD BLESS EVERYONE! @US_FDA @SteveFDA @CDCgov @DHSgov

Mar 23, 2020

WE CANNOT LET THE CURE
BE WORSE THAN THE PROBLEM
ITSELF. AT THE END OF THE 15 DAY
PERIOD, WE WILL MAKE A DECISION
AS TO WHICH WAY WE WANT TO GO!

Mar 24, 2020

THIS IS WHY WE NEED BORDERS!

Mar 25, 2020

Our people want to return to work. They will
practice Social Distancing and all else, and
Seniors will be watched over protectively &
lovingly. We can do two things together.
THE CURE CANNOT BE WORSE (by far)
THAN THE PROBLEM!
Congress MUST ACT NOW.
We will come back strong!

Mar 28, 2020

General Motors MUST immediately open their
stupidly abandoned Lordstown plant in
Ohio, or some other plant, and
START MAKING VENTILATORS, NOW!!!!!!
FORD, GET GOING ON
VENTILATORS, FAST!!!!!!

Mar 28, 2020

As usual with "this" General Motors,
things just never seem to work out.
They said they were going to give us 40,000
much needed Ventilators, "very quickly"
Now they are saying it will only be 6000,
in late April, and they want top dollar.
Always a mess with Mary B. Invoke "P".

Mar 28, 2020

Invoke "P" means Defense Production Act!

Mar 30, 2020

I am a great friend and admirer of the
Queen & the United Kingdom.
It was reported that Harry and Meghan,
who left the Kingdom, would reside
permanently in Canada. Now they have left
Canada for the U.S. however, the U.S.
will not pay for their security protection.
They must pay!

Apr 6, 2020

USA STRONG!

Apr 6, 2020

We are learning much about the
Invisible Enemy. It is tough and smart,
but we are tougher and smarter!

Apr 7, 2020

Joe Biden wanted the date for the Democrat
National Convention moved to a later time
period. Now he wants a "Virtual" Convention,
one where he doesn't have to show up.
Gee, I wonder why? Also, what ever happened
to that phone call he told the Fake News
he wanted to make to me?

Apr 8, 2020

The W.H.O. really blew it. For some reason,
funded largely by the United States,
yet very China centric. We will be giving that a
good look. Fortunately I rejected their advice
on keeping our borders open to
China early on. Why did they give us
such a faulty recommendation?

Apr 9, 2020

FLATTENING OF THE CURVE!

Apr 10, 2020

Great News: Prime Minister Boris Johnson
has just been moved out of Intensive Care.
Get well Boris!!!

Apr 11, 2020

The Invisible Enemy will soon be in full retreat!

Apr 12, 2020

So now the Fake News @nytimes is tracing the
CoronaVirus origins back to Europe,
NOT China. This is a first! I wonder
what the Failing New York Times
got for this one? Are there any
NAMED sources? They were recently thrown
out of China like dogs,
and obviously want back in. Sad!

Apr 13, 2020

I am working hard to expose the corruption
and dishonesty in the Lamestream Media.
That part is easy, the hard part is WHY?

Apr 15, 2020

GET RID OF BALLOT HARVESTING,
IT IS RAMPANT WITH FRAUD.
THE USA MUST HAVE VOTER I.D.,
THE ONLY WAY TO GET
AN HONEST COUNT!

Apr 15, 2020

Tell the Democrat Governors that
"Mutiny On The Bounty" was one of
my all time favorite movies. A good old
fashioned mutiny every now and then is an
exciting and invigorating thing to watch,
especially when the mutineers need
so much from the Captain. Too easy!

Apr 18, 2020

LIBERATE VIRGINIA, and save your great
2nd Amendment. It is under siege!

...

LIBERATE MICHIGAN!

...

LIBERATE MINNESOTA!

Apr 20, 2020

Just like I was right on Ventilators
(our Country is now the "King of Ventilators",
other countries are calling asking for
help-we will!), I am right on testing.
Governors must be able to
step up and get the job done.
We will be with you ALL THE WAY!

Apr 21, 2020

It is amazing that I became President of the
United States with such a totally corrupt
and dishonest Lamestream Media
going after me all day, and all night.
Either I'm really good, far better than the Fake
News wants to admit, or they don't have
nearly the power as once thought!

Apr 21, 2020

In light of the attack from the
Invisible Enemy, as well as the need
to protect the jobs of our
GREAT American Citizens,
I will be signing an Executive Order
to temporarily suspend immigration
into the United States!

Apr 22, 2020

States are safely coming back.
Our Country is starting to
OPEN FOR BUSINESS again.
Special care is, and always will be,
given to our beloved seniors (except me!).
Their lives will be better than ever ...
WE LOVE YOU ALL!

Apr 26, 2020

Was just informed that the Fake News
from the Thursday White House Press
Conference had me speaking & asking questions
of Dr. Deborah Birx. Wrong, I was speaking
to our Laboratory expert, not Deborah, about
sunlight etc. & the CoronaVirus.
The Lamestream Media is corrupt & sick!

Apr 27, 2020

The people that know me and know the
history of our Country say that I am the
hardest working President in history.
I don't know about that, but I am a
hard worker and have probably gotten
more done in the first 3 1/2 years than any
President in history. The Fake News hates it!

Apr 27, 2020

FAKE NEWS, THE ENEMY
OF THE PEOPLE!

Apr 29, 2020

The only reason the U.S. has reported one million cases of CoronaVirus is that our Testing is sooo much better than any other country in the World. Other countries are way behind us in Testing, and therefore show far fewer cases!

May 4, 2020

....And then came a Plague, a great and
powerful Plague, and the World was never
to be the same again! But America rose
from this death and destruction,
always remembering its many lost souls,
and the lost souls all over the World,
and became greater than ever before!

May 4, 2020

Intelligence has just reported to me that
I was correct, and that they did
NOT bring up the CoronaVirus subject matter
until late into January, just prior to
my banning China from the U.S. Also,
they only spoke of the Virus in a very
non-threatening, or matter of fact, manner...

....Fake News got it wrong again, as always,
and tens of thousands of lives were saved by
my EARLY BAN of China into our Country.
The people that we're allowed were heavily
scrutinized and tested U.S. citizens,
and as such, I welcome them with open arms!

May 7, 2020

The Fake News has reached an all time high!

May 10, 2020

TRANSITION TO GREATNESS!

May 10, 2020

We are getting great marks for the
handling of the CoronaVirus pandemic,
especially the very early BAN of people from
China, the infectious source, entering
the USA. Compare that to the Obama/Sleepy
Joe disaster known as H1N1 Swine Flu.
Poor marks, bad polls - didn't have a clue!

May 12, 2020

Asian Americans are VERY angry at
what China has done to our Country,
and the World. Chinese Americans are
the most angry of all. I don't blame them!

May 12, 2020

96% APPROVAL RATING IN THE
REPUBLICAN PARTY. THANK YOU!
We will win against a tired, exhausted man,
Sleepy Joe Biden, in November.

May 15, 2020

Thank you to all of my great
Keyboard Warriors. You are better,
and far more brilliant, than anyone on
Madison Avenue (Ad Agencies).
There is nobody like you!

May 16, 2020

We've done a GREAT job on
Covid response, making all Governors look
good, some fantastic (and that's OK),
but the Lamestream Media doesn't want
to go with that narrative, and the
Do Nothing Dems talking point is to
say only bad about "Trump"
Im ade everybody look good, but me!

May 18, 2020

REOPEN OUR COUNTRY!

May 20, 2020

Some wacko in China just released
a statement blaming everybody other than
China for the Virus which has now killed
hundreds of thousands of people.
Please explain to this dope that it was the
"incompetence of China", and nothing else,
that did this mass Worldwide killing!

May 21, 2020

Congratulations to my daughter,
Tiffany, on graduating from
Georgetown Law. Great student,
great school. Just what I need is a
lawyer in the family. Proud of you Tiff!

May 22, 2020

Is this even possible to believe?
Can this be for real?
Where is this nursing home,
how is the victim doing?

May 24, 2020

MAKE AMERICA GREAT AGAIN!

May 25, 2020

TRANSITION TO GREATNESS!
Get ready, it is already happening again!

May 26, 2020

There is NO WAY (ZERO!) that
Mail-In Ballots will be anything less than
substantially fraudulent. Mail boxes will be
robbed, ballots will be forged &
even illegally printed out &
fraudulently signed. The Governor of
California is sending Ballots to
millions of people, anyone.....

....living in the state, no matter who
they are or how they got there, will get one.
That will be followed up with professionals
telling all of these people, many of whom have
never even thought of voting before,
how, and for whom, to vote. This will be a
Rigged Election. No way!

Get the facts about mail-in ballots[1]

---

[1] This is the first instance of Twitter placing warnings on a @realDonaldTrump tweet. These boxes are direct quotes from the Twitter website.

May 27, 2020

.@Twitter is now interfering in the
2020 Presidential Election. They are saying
my statement on Mail-In Ballots, which
will lead to massive corruption and fraud, is
incorrect, based on fact-checking by
Fake News CNN and the
Amazon Washington Post....

....Twitter is completely stifling
FREE SPEECH, and I, as President,
will not allow it to happen!

May 28, 2020

Twitter has now shown that everything we
have been saying about them (and their other
compatriots) is correct. Big action to follow!

May 28, 2020

WARRANTLESS SURVEILLANCE OF
AMERICANS IS WRONG!

May 28, 2020

At my request, the FBI and the
Department of Justice are already well into an
investigation as to the very sad and tragic
death in Minnesota of George Floyd....

....I have asked for this investigation to be
expedited and greatly appreciate all of
the work done by local law enforcement.

May 28, 2020

This will be a Big Day for Social Media
and FAIRNESS!

May 29, 2020

All over the World the CoronaVirus, a very bad
"gift" from China, marches on. Not good!

May 29, 2020

So ridiculous to see Twitter trying
to make the case that Mail-In Ballots are not
subject to FRAUD. How stupid, there are
examples, & cases, all over the place.
Our election process will become
badly tainted & a laughingstock all over
the World. Tell that to your hater @yoyoel

May 29, 2020

.@Facebook CEO Mark Zuckerberg
is today criticizing Twitter. "We have a
different policy than Twitter on this.
I believe strongly that Facebook shouldn't be
the arbiter of truth of everything that
people say online." Did Twitter criticize
Obama for his "you can keep your Dr."?

May 29, 2020

MAIL-IN VOTING WILL LEAD TO
MASSIVE FRAUD AND ABUSE.
IT WILL ALSO LEAD TO THE END
OF OUR GREAT REPUBLICAN PARTY.
WE CAN NEVER LET THIS TRAGEDY
BEFALL OUR NATION.
BIG MAIL-IN VICTORY IN
TEXAS COURT TODAY. CONGRATS!!!

12:53am | May 29, 2020

I can't stand back & watch
this happen to a great
American City, Minneapolis.
A total lack of leadership. Either the
very weak Radical Left Mayor, Jacob Frey,
get his act together and bring the City under
control, or I will send in the National Guard
& get the job done right.....

...These THUGS are dishonoring
the memory of George Floyd,
and I won't let that happen. Just spoke to
Governor Tim Walz and told him that the
Military is with him all the way.
Any difficulty and we will assume control but,
when the looting starts, the shooting starts.
Thank you!

This Tweet violated the Twitter Rules
about glorifying violence. However,
Twitter has determined that it may be
in the public's interest for the
Tweet to remain accessible.

May 29, 2020

Twitter is doing nothing about all of the lies &
propaganda being put out by China
or the Radical Left Democrat Party.
They have targeted Republicans,
Conservatives & the President of the
United States. Section 230 should be
revoked by Congress. Until then,
it will be regulated!

May 29, 2020

CHINA!

May 30, 2020

The National Guard has arrived
on the scene. They are in Minneapolis
and fully prepared. George Floyd
will not have died in vain.
Respect his memory!!!

May 30, 2020

REVOKE 230!

May 31, 2020

These are "Organized Groups" that
have nothing to do with George Floyd. Sad!

May 31, 2020

It's ANTIFA and the Radical Left.
Don't lay the blame on others!

May 31, 2020

Hopefully a great, successful and safe
ROCKET LAUNCH. Lifting off soon!?!?
@FoxNews @OANN

Jun 1, 2020

FAKE NEWS!

Jun 1, 2020

NOVEMBER 3RD.

Jun 2, 2020

D.C. had no problems last night.
Many arrests. Great job done by all.
Overwhelming force. Domination.
Likewise, Minneapolis was great
(thank you President Trump!).

Jun 3, 2020

SILENT MAJORITY!

Jun 3, 2020

My Admin has done more for the
Black Community than any President since
Abraham Lincoln. Passed Opportunity Zones
with @SenatorTimScott, guaranteed funding
for HBCU's, School Choice, passed
Criminal Justice Reform,
lowest Black unemployment, poverty,
and crime rates in history...

Jun 3, 2020

Washington, D.C., was the safest place
on earth last night!

Jun 3, 2020

LAW & ORDER!

Jun 3, 2020

If you watch Fake News @CNN or
MSDNC, you would think that the killers,
terrorists, arsonists, anarchists, thugs,
hoodlums, looters, ANTIFA & others,
would be the nicest, kindest most wonderful
people in the Whole Wide World. No,
they are what they are –
very bad for our Country!

Jun 3, 2020

In 31/2 years, I've done much more for our Black population than Joe Biden has done in 43 years. Actually, he set them back big time with his Crime Bill, which he doesn't even remember. I've done more for Black Americans, in fact, than any President in U.S. history, with...

....the possible exception of another Republican President, the late, great, Abraham Lincoln ... and it's not even close. The Democrats know this, and so does the Fake News, but they refuse to write or say it because they are inherently corrupt! See "pinned" above.

Jun 5, 2020

YOU DON'T BURN CHURCHES IN AMERICA!

Jun 5, 2020

Really Big Jobs Report. Great going President Trump (kidding but true)!

Jun 8, 2020

Colin Powell, a real stiff who
was very responsible for getting us into
the disastrous Middle East Wars,
just announced he will be voting for
another stiff, Sleepy Joe Biden. Didn't
Powell say that Iraq had "weapons of
mass destruction?" They didn't,
but off we went to WAR!

Jun 9, 2020

Buffalo protester shoved by Police
could be an ANTIFA provocateur.
75 year old Martin Gugino was pushed away
after appearing to scan police communications
in order to black out the equipment.
@OANN I watched, he fell harder
than was pushed. Was aiming scanner.
Could be a set up?

Jun 12, 2020

THOSE THAT DENY THEIR HISTORY
ARE DOOMED TO REPEAT IT!

Jun 14, 2020

The ramp that I descended after my
West Point Commencement speech was very
long & steep, had no handrail and,
most importantly, was very slippery.
The last thing I was going to do is "fall"
for the Fake News to have fun with.
Final ten feet I ran down to level ground.
Momentum!

Jun 15, 2020

Almost One Million people request tickets for
the Saturday Night Rally in Tulsa, Oklahoma!

Jun 16, 2020

Our testing is so much bigger and more
advanced than any other country
(we have done a great job on this!)
that it shows more cases. Without testing, or
weak testing, we would be showing almost no
cases. Testing is a double edged sword -
Makes us look bad, but good to have!!!

Jun 18, 2020

Wacko John Bolton's "exceedingly tedious"
(New York Times) book is made up of lies &
fake stories. Said all good about me, in print,
until the day I fired him. A disgruntled
boring fool who only wanted to go to war.
Never had a clue, was ostracized &
happily dumped. What a dope!

Jun 19, 2020

When Wacko John Bolton went on
Deface the Nation and so stupidly said that
he looked at the "Libyan Model" for
North Korea, all hell broke out. Kim Jong Un,
who we were getting along with very well,
went "ballistic", just like his missiles -
and rightfully so....

....He didn't want Bolton anywhere near him.
Bolton's dumbest of all statements set us back
very badly with North Korea, even now.
I asked him, "what the hell were you thinking?"
He had no answer and just apologized.
That was early on, I should have fired him
right then & there!

Jun 19, 2020

Do you get the impression that the
Supreme Court doesn't like me?

Jun 19, 2020

First thing the anarchists did upon
taking over Seattle was "BUILD A WALL"
See, I was ahead of our times!

Jun 23, 2020

There will never be an "Autonomous Zone"
in Washington, D.C., as long as
I'm your President. If they try they will
be met with serious force!

*This Tweet violated the Twitter Rules
about abusive behavior. However,
Twitter has determined that it may be in the
public's interest for the Tweet to remain accessible.*

Jun 25, 2020

Pres. Obama destroyed the lobster
and fishing industry in Maine. Now it's back,
bigger and better than anyone ever thought
possible. Enjoy your "lobstering"
and fishing! Make lots of money!

Jun 28, 2020

Funny to see Corrupt Joe Biden reading
a statement on Russia, which was obviously
written by his handlers. Russia ate his and
Obama's lunch during their time in office,
so badly that Obama wanted them out of the
then G-8. U.S. was weak on everything,
but especially Russia!

Jun 28, 2020

THE VAST SILENT MAJORITY IS
ALIVE AND WELL!!! We will win this
Election big. Nobody wants a Low IQ
person in charge of our Country, and
Sleepy Joe is definitely a Low IQ person!

Jul 26, 2020

Crazy Nancy Pelosi said I made a
mistake when I banned people from infected
China from entering the U.S. in January.
Tens of thousands of lives were saved,
as she danced in the Streets of
Chinatown (SF) in late February.
Biden agreed with her, but soon
admitted that I was right!

Jul 28, 2020

So disgusting to watch Twitter's so-called
"Trending", where sooo many trends are
about me, and never a good one.
They look for anything they can find,
make it as bad as possible, and blow it up,
trying to make it trend. Really ridiculous,
illegal, and, of course, very unfair!

Aug 1, 2020

We have more Cases because we do more
Testing. It's Lamestream Media Gold!

Aug 4, 2020

OPEN THE SCHOOLS!!!

Aug 4, 2020

My visits last week to Texas and
Florida had massive numbers of cheering
people gathered along the roads and highways,
thousands and thousands, even bigger
(by far) than the crowds of 2016. Saw no
Biden supporters, and yet some in the
Fake News said it was an equal number. Sad!

Aug 4, 2020

People are not happy that players are not
standing for our National Anthem!

Aug 5, 2020

Nevada has ZERO infrastructure for
Mail-In Voting. It will be a corrupt disaster
if not ended by the Courts. It will take months,
or years, to figure out. Florida has built a great
infrastructure, over years, with
two great Republican Governors. Florida,
send in your Ballots!

Aug 6, 2020

How can voters be sending in Ballots starting,
in some cases, one month before the
First Presidential Debate. Move the
First Debate up. A debate, to me,
is a Public Service. Joe Biden and
I owe it to the American People!

Aug 7, 2020

After yesterday's statement, Sleepy Joe Biden is
no longer worthy of the Black Vote!

Aug 7, 2020

Great Jobs Numbers!

Aug 10, 2020

So now Schumer and Pelosi want to meet to
make a deal. Amazing how it all works,
isn't it. Where have they been for the
last 4 weeks when they were "hardliners",
and only wanted BAILOUT MONEY for
Democrat run states and cities that are failing
badly? They know my phone number!

Aug 11, 2020

Play College Football!

Aug 13, 2020

Very poor morning TV ratings for
MSDNC's Morning Joe, headed by a
complete Psycho named Joe Scarborough
and his ditzy airhead wife, Mika, and also
@CNN, headed by complete unknowns.
Congratulations to @foxandfriends on
dominating the mornings
(thank you President Trump!).

Aug 15, 2020

I haave directed @stevemmnuchin1
to get ready to send direct payments
($3,400 for family of four) to all Americans.
DEMOCRATS ARE HOLDING THIS UP!

Aug 15, 2020

I am ready to have @USTreasury and @
SBA send additional PPP payments to
small businesses that have been hurt by the
ChinaVirus. DEMOCRATS ARE
HOLDING THIS UP!

Aug 15, 2020

I am ready to send more money to
States and Local governments to save jobs
for Police, Fire Fighters, First Responders,
and Teachers. DEMOCRATS
ARE HOLDING THIS UP!

Aug 15, 2020

I am ready to send $105B to the states
to help open schools safely with
additional PPE. DEMOCRATS ARE
HOLDING THIS UP!

Aug 15, 2020

I am ready to send Rental Assistance
payments to hardworking Americans
that have been hurt by the ChinaVirus.
DEMOCRATS ARE HOLDING THIS UP!

Aug 15, 2020

The biggest difference between the
Presidential Race in 2020 and that of 2016
is the 2016 candidate, Crooked Hillary Clinton,
was much smarter and sharper than Slow Joe,
we have even more ENTHUSIASM now,
and @FoxNews has become politically
correct and no longer the big deal!

Aug 18, 2020

SAVE THE POST OFFICE!

Aug 18, 2020

The ObamaBiden Administration was the
most corrupt in history, including the fact that
they got caught SPYING ON MY
CAMPAIGN, the biggest political scandal
in the history of our Country.
It's called Treason, and more.
Thanks for your very kind words Michelle!

Aug 19, 2020

People forget how divided our
Country was under ObamaBiden.
The anger and hatred were unbelievable.
They shouldn't be lecturing to us. I'm here,
as your President, because of them!

Aug 19, 2020

IF YOU CAN PROTEST IN PERSON,
YOU CAN VOTE IN PERSON!

Aug 20, 2020

Don't buy GOODYEAR TIRES - They
announced a BAN ON MAGA HATS.
Get better tires for far less!
(This is what the Radical Left Democrats do.
Two can play the same game,
and we have to start playing it now!).

Aug 20, 2020

HE SPIED ON MY CAMPAIGN,
AND GOT CAUGHT!

Aug 20, 2020

WHY DID HE REFUSE TO ENDORSE
SLOW JOE UNTIL IT WAS ALL OVER,
AND EVEN THEN WAS VERY LATE?
WHY DID HE TRY TO GET HIM
NOT TO RUN?

Aug 20, 2020

BUT DIDN'T SHE CALL HIM A RACIST???
DIDN'T SHE SAY
HE WAS INCOMPETENT???

Aug 21, 2020

The Democrats are demanding Mail-In
Ballots because the enthusiasm meter for
Slow Joe Biden is the lowest in recorded
history, and they are concerned that very few
people will turn out to vote. Instead,
they will search & find people, then "harvest"
& return Ballots. Not fair!

Aug 21, 2020

To get into the Democrat National Convention,
you must have an ID card with a picture ...
Yet the Democrats refuse to do this when
it come to your very important VOTE! Gee,
I wonder WHY???

Aug 22, 2020

Robert, I Love You. Rest In Peace!

Aug 23, 2020

So now the Democrats are using
Mail Drop Boxes, which are a voter security
disaster. Among other things, they make it
possible for a person to vote multiple times.
Also, who controls them, are they placed in
Republican or Democrat areas?
They are not Covid sanitized.
A big fraud!

*This Tweet violated the Twitter Rules about
civic and election integrity. However,
Twitter has determined that it may be in the
public's interest for the Tweet to remain accessible.*

Aug 30, 2020

Now that Biden's Polls are dropping fast,
he has agreed to get out of his basement
and start campaignin;'in ten days:'
Sadly, that is a very slow reaction time for a
President. Our beloved USA needs a
much faster, smarter, and tougher
response than that. Get out there today, Joe!

Sep 2, 2020

It never ends! Now they are trying
to say that your favorite President, me,
went to Walter Reed Medical Center,
having suffered a series of ministrokes.
Never happened to THIS candidate -
FAKE NEWS. Perhaps they are referring to
another candidate from another Party!

Sep 2, 2020

Crazy Nancy Pelosi is being decimated
for having a beauty parlor opened,
when all others are closed, and for
not wearing a Mask – despite constantly
lecturing everyone else. We will almost
certainly take back the House,
and send Nancy packing!

Sep 3, 2020

"The Dow Jones Industrial just closed above
29,000! You are so lucky to have me
as your President ☺ With Joe Hiden'
it would crash ☹ "

Sep 4, 2020

Nancy Pelosi says she got "set up"
by a Beauty Parlor owner. Maybe the
Beauty Parlor owner should be running
the House of Representatives instead of
Crazy Nancy?

Sep 7, 2020

Biden Underperforming! @OANN
What else is new, the story of his life.

Sep 8, 2020

Just heard that Wacko John Bolton
was talking of the fact that I discussed "love
letters from Kim Jong Un" as though I viewed
them as just that. Obviously, was just being
sarcastic. Bolton was such a jerk!

Sep 8, 2020

Biggest & Fastest Financial Recovery
In History. Next year will be BEST EVER,
unless a very Sleepy person becomes
President and massively raises your taxes -
In which case, CRASH!

Sep 8, 2020

The Real Polls are starting to look GREAT!
We will be having an even bigger victory than
that of 2016. The Radical Left Anarchists,
Agitators, Looters, and just plain Lunatics,
will not be happy, but they will behave!

Sep 9, 2020

Suburban voters are pouring into the
Republican Party because of the violence in
Democrat run cities and states. If Biden gets in,
this violence is "coming to the Suburbs",
and FAST. You could say goodbye to
your American Dream!

Sep 10, 2020

Kim Jong Un is in good health.
Never underestimate him!

Sep 11, 2020

Congratulations to JPMorgan Chase for
ordering everyone BACK TO OFFICE on
September 21st. Will always be better than
working from home!

Sep 12, 2020

ALERT: So now we find out that the entire Mueller "hit squad" illegally wiped their phones clean just prior to the investigation of them, all using the same really dumb reason for this "accident", just like Crooked Hillary smashing her phones with a hammer, & DELETING HER EMAILS!

Sep 12, 2020

NORTH CAROLINA: To make sure your Ballot COUNTS, sign & send it in EARLY. When Polls open, go to your Polling Place to see if it was COUNTED. IF NOT, VOTE! Your signed Ballot will not count because your vote has been posted. Don't let them illegally take your vote away from you!

This Tweet violated the Twitter Rules about civic and election integrity. However, Twitter has determined that it may be in the public's interest for the Tweet to remain accessible.

Sep 13, 2020

While It ravel the Country, Joe sleeps in his
basement, telling the Fake News Media to
"get lost" If you're a reporter covering
Sleepy Joe, you have basically gone
into retirement!

Sep 14, 2020

Sleepy Joe Biden has spent 47 years in
politics being terrible to Hispanics. Now he
is relying on Castro lover Bernie Sanders
to help him out. That won't work!
Remember, Miami Cubans gave me the highly
honored Bay of Pigs Award for all
I have done for our great Cuban Population!

Sep 13, 2020

I am running for re-election to bring
prosperity to Nevada, to put violent criminals
behind bars, and to ensure the future belongs
to AMERICA—NOT China. If we win,
AMERICA WINS! If Biden wins, China wins.
If Biden Wins, the rioters, anarchists, and
arsonists win. VOTE! #MAGA

Sep 17, 2020

The big Unsolicited Ballot States
should give it up NOW, before it is too late,
and ask people to go to the
Polling Booths and, like always before, VOTE.
Otherwise, MAYHEM!!! Solicited Ballots
(absentee) are OK. @foxandfriends

Learn how voting by mail is safe and secure

Sep 17, 2020

Twitter makes sure that Trending on
Twitter is anything bad, Fake or not,
about President Donald Trump.
So obvious what they are doing.
Being studied now!

Sep 18, 2020

Unsolicited Ballots are
uncontrollable, totally open to
ELECTION INTERFERENCE
by foreign countries, and will lead to
massive chaos and confusion!

Learn how voting by mail is safe and secure

Sep 19, 2020

Mini Mike Bloomberg,
after making a total fool of himself as
he got badly beaten up by Pocahontas
and the Democrats in the Primaries,
is at it again. He tried to buy an Election
and went away with a major
case of Depression. Now he's throwing
money at the Dems, looking for a job!

Sep 20, 2020

.@GOP We were put in this position of
power and importance to make decisions
for the people who so proudly elected us,
the most important of which has long
been considered to be the selection of
United States Supreme Court Justices.
We have this obligation, without delay!

Sep 23, 2020

I hardly know Cindy McCain other
than having put her on a Committee at her
husband's request. Joe Biden was
John McCain's lapdog. So many
BAD decisions on Endless Wars & the V.A.,
which Ib rought from a horror show to
HIGH APPROVAL. Never a fan of John.
Cindy can have Sleepy Joe!

Sep 24, 2020

LAW & ORDER!

Sep 25, 2020

Russian Billionaire wired
Hunter Biden 31/2 Million Dollars.
This on top of all of the other money
he received while Joe was V.P. Crooked
as can be, but Fake Mainstream Media
wants it to just go away!

Sep 27, 2020

I will be strongly demanding a
Drug Test of Sleepy Joe Biden prior to,
or after, the Debate on Tuesday night.
Naturally, I will agree to take one also.
His Debate performances have been record
setting UNEVEN, to put it mildly. Only drugs
could have caused this discrepancy???

Sep 28, 2020

WATCH THE BALLOTS!!!

Sep 28, 2020

FAKE NEWS!

Sep 29, 2020

Joe Biden just announced that he will
not agree to a Drug Test. Gee, I wonder why?

Oct 1, 2020

100,000 DEFECTIVE BALLOTS
IN NEW YORK. THEY WANT TO
REPLACE THEM, BUT WHERE,
AND WHAT HAPPENS TO,
THE BALLOTS THAT WERE
FIRST SENT? THEY WILL BE USED
BY SOMEBODY. USA, END THIS
SCAM - GO OUT AND VOTE!

Oct 1, 2020

So when will something significant
happen to James Comey? Got caught cold.
He is either very dumb, or one of the
worst liars in political history. TOO LONG.
EMBARRASSING!

Oct 2, 2020

I won the debate big, based on
compilation of polls etc. Thank you!

Oct 2, 2020

Hope Hicks, who has been working
so hard without even taking a small break,
has just tested positive for Covid 19. Terrible!
The First Lady and I are waiting for our
test results. In the meantime, we will
begin our quarantine process!

Oct 2, 2020

Tonight, @FLOTUS and I tested positive
for COVID-19. We will begin our quarantine
and recovery process immediately.
We will get through this TOGETHER!

Oct 3, 2020

Going well, I think!
Thank you to all. LOVE!!!

Oct 4, 2020

Doctors, Nurses and ALL at the
GREAT Walter Reed Medical Center,
and others from likewise incredible institutions
who have joined them, are AMAZING!!!
Tremendous progress has been made over
the last 6 months in fighting this PLAGUE.
With their help, I am feeling well!

Oct 5, 2020

I really appreciate all of the fans and
supporters outside of the hospital.
The fact is, they really love our Country
and are seeing how we are MAKING IT
GREATER THAN EVER BEFORE!

Oct 5, 2020

STOCK MARKET HIGHS. VOTE!

Oct 5, 2020

STRONGEST EVER MILITARY. VOTE!

Oct 5, 2020

LAW & ORDER. VOTE!

Oct 5, 2020

RELIGIOUS LIBERTY. VOTE!

Oct 5, 2020

BIGGEST TAX CUT EVER, AND
ANOTHER ONE COMING. VOTE!

Oct 5, 2020

401(K). VOTE!

Oct 5, 2020

BEST V.A. EVER. 91%
APPROVAL RATING. VOTE!

Oct 5, 2020

SPACE FORCE. VOTE!

Oct 5, 2020

MASSIVE REGULATION CUTS. VOTE!

Oct 5, 2020

PRO LIFE! VOTE!

Oct 5, 2020

BETTER & CHEAPER HEALTHCARE.
VOTE!

Oct 5, 2020

PROTECT PREEXISTING CONDITIONS.
VOTE!

Oct 5, 2020

FIGHT THE CORRUPT FAKE NEWS
MEDIA. VOTE!

Oct 5, 2020

SAVE OUR SECOND AMENDMENT.
VOTE!

Oct 5, 2020

PEACE THROUGH STRENGTH
(BRING OUR SOLDIERS HOME). VOTE!

Oct 6, 2020

I will be leaving the great Walter Reed
Medical Center today at 6:30 P.M.
Feeling really good! Don't be afraid of Covid.
Don't let it dominate your life. We have
developed, under the Trump Administration,
some really great drugs & knowledge.
I feel better than I did 20 years ago!

Oct 6, 2020

It is reported that the Media is upset because I got into a secure vehicle to say thank you to the many fans and supporters who were standing outside of the hospital for many hours, and even days, to pay their respect to their President. If I didn't do it, Media would say RUDE!!

Oct 6, 2020

Flu season is coming up! Many people every year, sometimes over 100,000, and despite the Vaccine, die from the Flu. Are we going to close down our Country? No, we have learned to live with it, just like we are learning to live with Covid, in most populations far less lethal!!!

This Tweet violated the Twitter Rules about spreading misleading and potentially harmful information related to COVID-19. However, Twitter has determined that it may be in the public's interest for the Tweet to remain accessible.

Oct 7, 2020

FEELING GREAT!

Oct 7, 2020

Mini Mike Bloomberg, who made a
fool of himself on the Dems debate stage
when Elizabeth Warren & the others
simply took him apart, is going "crazy"
trying to buy his way back into the Liberal
Democrat's hearts. His Florida ads are lies.
I am much better for SENIORS than Sleepy!

Oct 7, 2020

How does Biden lead in Pennsylvania Polls
when he is against Fracking (JOBS!),
2nd Amendment and Religion? Fake Polls.
I will win Pennsylvania!

Oct 7, 2020

New FDA Rules make it more difficult
for them to speed up vaccines for approval
before Election Day. Just another
political hit job! @SteveFDA

Oct 8, 2020

THE FAKE NEWS MEDIA IS THE
REAL OPPOSITION PARTY!

Oct 8, 2020

Mike Pence is doing GREAT!
She is a gaffe machine.

Oct 9, 2020

If a Republican LIED like Biden and
Harris do, constantly, the Lamestream Media
would be calling them out at a level never
recorded before. For one year they called for
No Fracking and big Tax Increases.
Now they each say opposite.
Fake News is working overtime!

Oct 9, 2020

Joe Biden has no plan for Coronavirus -
ALL TALK! He was a disaster in his
handling of H1N1 Swine Flu.
He didn't have a clue, with his own
Chief of Staff so saying. If he were in charge,
perhaps 2.2 million people would have died
from this much more lethal disease!

Oct 9, 2020

Biden is against Oil, Guns and Religion,
a very bad combination to be fighting
in the Great State of Texas. We are
Winning Big, in the Real Polls, all over the
Country!!! NOVEMBER 3rd. VOTE!!!

Oct 10, 2020

Steve Scully, the second Debate Moderator,
is a Never Trumper, just like the son of the
great Mike Wallace. Fix!!!

Oct 10, 2020

Crazy Nancy Pelosi is looking at the
25th Amendment in order to replace
Joe Biden with Kamala Harris.
The Dems want that to happen fast because
Sleepy Joe is out of it!!!

Oct 11, 2020

Joe Biden is a PUPPET of
CASTRO-CHAVISTAS like Crazy Bernie,
AOC and Castro-lover Karen Bass. Biden is
supported by socialist Gustavo Petro,
a major LOSER and former M-19 guerrilla
leader. Biden is weak on socialism and
will betray Colombia. I stand with you!

Oct 12, 2020

California is going to hell. Vote Trump!

Oct 12, 2020

New York has gone to hell. Vote Trump!

Oct 12, 2020

Illinois has no place to go. Sad, isn't it?
Vote Trump!

Oct 13, 2020

We will have Healthcare which is
FAR BETTER than ObamaCare, at a
FAR LOWER COST - BIG PREMIUM
REDUCTION. PEOPLE WITH PRE
EXISTING CONDITIONS WILL BE
PROTECTED AT AN EVEN
HIGHER LEVEL THAN NOW.
HIGHLY UNPOPULAR AND UNFAIR
INDIVIDUAL MANDATE ALREADY
TERMINATED. YOU'RE WELCOME!

Oct 13, 2020

Sleepy Joe Biden had a particularly
bad day today. He couldn't remember
the name of Mitt Romney, said again
he was running for the U.S. Senate,
and forgot what State he was in.
If I did any of this, it would be disqualifying.
With him, he's just Sleepy Joe!

Oct 13, 2020

What's going on, almost nobody
is showing up for Sleepy Joe rallies!

Oct 16, 2020

Big T was not a reference to me,
but rather to Big Tech, which should
have been properly pointed out in
Twitter's Fake Trending Section!

Oct 17, 2020

Biden made another big mistake. He totally
mixed up two Crime Bills. Didn't have a clue
(as usual!). Also, he freely used the term
SUPER PREDATOR!!!

Oct 20, 2020

Dr.Tony Fauci says we don't allow him to do
television, and yet I saw him last night on
@60Minutes, and he seems to get more
airtime than anybody since the late, great,
Bob Hope. All I ask of Tony is that he make
better decisions. He said "no masks & let
China in". Also, Bad arm!

Oct 24, 2020

Joe Biden was very disrespectful to
President Obama at last night's debate
when he said that he, Joe,
"was Vice President, not President,"
when trying to make excuses for their failed
immigration policies. I wonder what "O"
was thinking when he heard that one?

Oct 25, 2020

JUST VOTED. A great honor!

Oct 26, 2020

Have a GREAT "MAGA-GRAS"
Rally today on our wonderful Long Island.
Cut Taxes, Stop Crime, VOTE FOR TRUMP.
Our City and State are a MESS.
What do you have to lose? Thank you!!!

Oct 26, 2020

Congratulations to Armenian
Prime Minister Nikol Pashinyan and
Azerbaijani President Ilham Aliyev,
who just agreed to adhere to a cease fire
effective at midnight. Many lives will be saved.
Proud of my team @SecPompeo &
Steve Biegun & @WHNSC
for getting the deal done!

Oct 26, 2020

Joe Biden called me George yesterday.
Couldn't remember my name.
Got some help from the anchor to get him
through the interview. The Fake News Cartel
is working overtime to cover it up!

Oct 26, 2020

The Fake News Media is riding COVID,
COVID, COVID, all the way to the Election.
Losers!

Oct 27, 2020

Strongly Trending (Google) since immediately after the second debate is CAN I CHANGE MY VOTE? This refers changing it to me. The answer in most states is YES. Go do it. Most important Election of your life!

Oct 27, 2020

ALL THE FAKE NEWS MEDIA WANTS TO TALK ABOUT IS COVID, COVID, COVID. ON NOVEMBER 4th, YOU WON'T BE HEARING SO MUCH ABOUT IT ANYMORE. WE ARE ROUNDING THE TURN!!!

Oct 27, 2020

7 DAYS!!!

Oct 27, 2020

MAKE AMERICA GREAT AGAIN!

Oct 28, 2020

They (his handlers) ripped Sleepy Joe off the stage yesterday when he got lost in a "mental fog". A disaster. Very little reporting on this!

Oct 28, 2020

Joe Biden is a corrupt politician. He wants to send YOUR jobs to China, while his family rakes in millions from the Chinese Communist Party. If Biden wins, China will OWN the USA. When we win, YOU win, Wisconsin wins, and AMERICA wins! #VOTE

Oct 28, 2020

As a developer long ago, and continuing to this day, the politicians ran Chicago into the ground. I was able to make an appropriately great deal with the numerous lenders on a large and very beautiful tower. Doesn't that make me a smart guy rather than a bad guy?

Oct 29, 2020

The USA doesn't have Freedom of the Press,
we have Suppression of the Story,
or just plain Fake News. So much has been
learned in the last two weeks about
how corrupt our Media is, and now Big Tech,
maybe even worse. Repeal Section 230!

Oct 30, 2020

#BidenCrimeFamiily

Oct 31, 2020

President Obama used to say that
"if you wanted to see something really
screwed up, give it to Joe Biden to do."
In fact, he tried to keep Joe from running,
"you don't have to do this Joe", and then
wouldn't endorse him until long after the
Primaries ended. "Joe is lost!".

Oct 31, 2020

MAKE AMERICA GREAT AGAIN!

Nov 1, 2020

Last night, our Country's brave warriors
rescued an American hostage in Nigeria. Our
Nation salutes the courageous soldiers behind
the daring nighttime rescue operation and
celebrates the safe return of
yet another American citizen!

Nov 1, 2020

Joe Biden called Black Youth
SUPER PREDATORS. They will
NEVER like him, or vote for him.
They are voting for "TRUMP".

Nov 2, 2020

The legendary actor, 007 Sean Connery,
has past on to even greener fairways.
He was quite a guy, and a tough character.
I was having a very hard time getting approvals
for a big development in Scotland when
Sean stepped in and shouted, "Let him build
the damn thing". That was....

....all I needed, everything went swimmingly
from there. He was so highly regarded &
respected in Scotland and beyond that years of
future turmoil was avoided. Sean was a
great actor and an even greater man.
Sincere condolences to his family!

Nov 2, 2020

For decades, Joe Biden let other countries
rip you off and cheat America blind!
The only people who've benefited from his
policies are himself & his family.
He shows up every 4 years, and then goes
back to D.C. and caters to his special interests.
My only special interest is YOU.

Nov 2, 2020

Biden will terminate school choice,
eliminate charter schools, defund religious
schools, ban prayer in public schools,
indoctrinate your children with Anti-American
lies, and force you to subsidize extreme
late-term abortion. We believe that every
child is a Sacred Gift from God!

Nov 2, 2020

Joe Biden is the candidate of rioters, looters,
arsonists, gun-grabbers, flag-burners,
Marxists, lobbyists, and special interests.
I am the candidate of farmers,
factory workers, police officers, and
hard-working, law-abiding patriots of
every race, religion and creed! #MAGA

Nov 2, 2020

The Depraved Swamp have been trying to
stop me – because they know I don't answer to
THEM – I answer only to YOU. Together,
we will defeat the corrupt establishment,
we will DETHRONE the failed political class,
we will drain the Washington Swamp &
we will SAVE THE AMERICAN DREAM!

Nov 2, 2020

Joe Biden is a globalist who spent
47 years outsourcing your jobs, opening
your borders, and sacrificing American blood
and treasure in endless foreign wars.
He shuttered your steel mills,
annihilated your coal jobs, and supported
every disastrous trade deal for half a century...

...He was a cheerleader for NAFTA and
China's entry into the WTO.
Pennsylvania lost half of its manufacturing jobs
after those Biden Calamities.
Joe Biden is a corrupt politician who
SOLD OUT Pennsylvania to CHINA!

Nov 2, 2020

Joe Biden is promising to delay the vaccine
and turn America into a prison state—
locking you in your home while letting far-left
rioters roam free. The Biden Lockdown will
mean no school, no graduations, no weddings,
no Thanksgiving, no Christmas,
no Fourth of July, and...

...no future for America's youth.
A vote for Biden is a vote for Lockdowns,
Layoffs and Misery.
Get out and VOTE tomorrow!

Nov 3, 2020

WE ARE LOOKING REALLY GOOD ALL
OVER THE COUNTRY. THANK YOU!

Nov 3, 2020

I will be making a statement tonight.
A big WIN!

Nov 3, 2020

We are up BIG, but they are trying to STEAL the Election. We will never let them do it. Votes cannot be cast after the Polls are closed!

Some or all of the content shared in this Tweet is disputed and might be misleading about an election or other civic process.

Nov 4, 2020

Last night I was leading, often solidly,
in many key States, in almost
all instances Democrat run & controlled.
Then, one by one, they started to
magically disappear as surprise ballot dumps
were counted. VERY STRANGE,
and the "pollsters" got it completely &
historically wrong!

Nov 5, 2020

They are finding Biden votes all over
the place — in Pennsylvania, Wisconsin, and
Michigan. So bad for our Country!

Nov 5, 2020

We have claimed, for Electoral Vote
purposes, the Commonwealth of
Pennsylvania (which won't allow
legal observers) the State of Georgia,
and the State of North Carolina,
each one of which has a BIG Trump lead.
Additionally, we hereby claim the
State of Michigan if, in fact,.....

.....there was a large number of
secretly dumped ballots as has been
widely reported!

*Official sources may not have called the race
when this was Tweeted*

Nov 6, 2020

STOP THE COUNT!

Nov 6, 2020

Big legal win in Pennsylvania!

STOP THE FRAUD!

Some or all of the content shared in this Tweet is disputed and might be misleading about an election or other civic process.

I easily WIN the Presidency of the United States with LEGAL VOTES CAST. The OBSERVERS were not allowed, in any way, shape, or form, to do their job and therefore, votes accepted during this period must be determined to be ILLEGAL VOTES. U.S. Supreme Court should decide!

Some or all of the content shared in this Tweet is disputed and might be misleading about an election or other civic process.

Nov 6, 2020

Twitter is out of control, made possible
through the government gift of Section 230!

Nov 7, 2020

Joe Biden should not wrongfully claim
the office of the President. I could make
that claim also. Legal proceedings
are just now beginning!

Nov 8, 2020

Big press conference today in Philadelphia at
Four Seasons Total Landscaping — 11:30am!

Nov 8, 2020

I WON THIS ELECTION, BY A LOT!

*Official sources may not have called the race
when this was Tweeted*

Nov 8, 2020

THE OBSERVERS WERE NOT ALLOWED
INTO THE COUNTING ROOMS.
I WON THE ELECTION,
GOT 71,000,000 LEGAL VOTES.
BAD THINGS HAPPENED WHICH OUR
OBSERVERS WERE NOT ALLOWED
TO SEE. NEVER HAPPENED BEFORE.
MILLIONS OF MAIL-IN BALLOTS
WERE SENT TO PEOPLE WHO
NEVER ASKED FOR THEM!

This claim about election fraud is disputed

Nov 9, 2020

Since when does the Lamestream Media
call who our next president will be?
We have all learned a lot in the last two weeks!

Nov 11, 2020

WE WILL WIN!

Nov 11, 2020

WATCH FOR MASSIVE BALLOT
COUNTING ABUSE AND,
JUST LIKE THE EARLY VACCINE,
REMEMBER I TOLD YOU SO!

Nov 13, 2020

"REPORT: DOMINION DELETED
2.7 MILLION TRUMP VOTES
NATIONWIDE. DATA ANALYSIS
FINDS 221,000 PENNSYLVANIA VOTES
SWITCHED FROM PRESIDENT TRUMP
TO BIDEN. 941,000 TRUMP VOTES
DELETED. STATES USING DOMINION
VOTING SYSTEMS SWITCHED 435,000
VOTES FROM TRUMP TO BIDEN."
@ChanelRion @OANN

This claim about election fraud is disputed

Nov 16, 2020

John Bolton was one of the dumbest people in government that I've had the "pleasure" to work with. A sullen, dull and quiet guy, he added nothing to National Security except, "Gee, let's go to war." Also, illegally released much Classified Information. A real dope!

Nov 16, 2020

I WON THE ELECTION!

Election officials have certified Joe Biden as the winner of the U.S. Presidential election

Nov 17, 2020

I won the Election!

Election officials have certified Joe Biden as the winner of the U.S. Presidential election

Nov 19, 2020

In Detroit, there are FAR MORE VOTES
THAN PEOPLE. Nothing can be done to
cure that giant scam. I win Michigan!
This claim about election fraud is disputed

Nov 19, 2020

VACCINES ARE COMING FAST!!!

Nov 20, 2020

THE COVID DRUGS NOW AVAILABLE
TO MAKE PEOPLE BETTER ARE
AMAZING, BUT SELDOM TALKED
ABOUT BY THE MEDIA!
Mortality rate is 85% down!

11:07 | Nov 23, 2020

What does GSA being allowed to
preliminarily work with the Dems have to do
with continuing to pursue our various cases on
what will go down as the most corrupt election
in American political history? We are
moving full speed ahead. Will never concede
to fake ballots & "Dominion".

Nov 25, 2020

Should President Trump concede to Biden?
Poll Results: No: 190,593 (98.9%)
Yes: 2,181 (1.1%) Total Votes: 192,774.
@gregkellyusa @newsmax For the good
of our Country we must prevail!

Nov 26, 2020

It is my Great Honor to announce that
General Michael T. Flynn has been granted a
Full Pardon. Congratulations to
@GenFlynn and his wonderful family,
I know you will now have a
truly fantastic Thanksgiving!

Nov 26, 2020

The "losers & suckers" statement on dead military heroes has been proven to be a total fabrication and lie. IT WAS NEVER MADE! The "anonymous" fabricator, who is a major sleaze, went forward with the lie despite 25 strong witnesses to the contrary. Welcome to the roaring 20's!

11:06 pm | Nov 26, 2020

Twitter is sending out totally false "Trends" that have absolutely nothing to do with what is really trending in the world. They make it up, and only negative "stuff". Same thing will happen to Twitter as is happening to @FoxNews daytime. Also, big Conservative discrimination!

Nov 28, 2020

Biden can only enter the White House as President if he can prove that his ridiculous "80,000,000 votes" were not fraudulently or illegally obtained. When you see what happened in Detroit, Atlanta, Philadelphia & Milwaukee, massive voter fraud, he's got a big unsolvable problem!

This claim about election fraud is disputed

Dec 1, 2020

I'm not fighting for me, I'm fighting for the
74,000,000 million people (not including the
many Trump ballots that were "tossed"),
a record for a sitting President,
who voted for me!

Dec 10, 2020

#OVERTURN

Dec 10, 2020

Wow! At least 17 States have joined
Texas in the extraordinary case against the
greatest Election Fraud in the history of the
United States. Thank you!

This claim about election fraud is disputed

Dec 11, 2020

WISDOM & COURAGE!!!

Dec 11, 2020

Morocco recognized the United States
in 1777. It is thus fitting we recognize
their sovereignty over the Western Sahara.

Dec 11, 2020

I just want to stop the world from killing itself!

Dec 11, 2020

Now it turns out that my phone call
to the President of Ukraine, which many,
including me, have called "perfect",
was even better than that. I predicted Biden
corruption, said to call the A.G.,
who perhaps knew of the corruption
during the impeachment hoax?

Dec 13, 2020

I WON THE ELECTION IN
A LANDSLIDE, but remember,
I only think in terms of legal votes,
not all of the fake voters and fraud that
miraculously floated in from everywhere!
What a disgrace!

This claim about election fraud is disputed

Dec 13, 2020

WE HAVE JUST BEGUN TO FIGHT!!!

Dec 14, 2020

Vaccines are shipped and on their way,
FIVE YEARS AHEAD OF SCHEDULE.
Get well USA. Get well WORLD.
We love you all!

Dec 15, 2020

First Vaccine Administered.
Congratulations USA!
Congratulations WORLD!

Dec 16, 2020

Poll: 92% of Republican Voters
think the election was rigged!

Dec 25, 2020

Twitter is going wild with their flags,
trying hard to suppress even the truth.
Just shows how dangerous they are,
purposely stifling free speech.
Very dangerous for our Country.
Does Congress know that this is how
Communism starts? Cancel Culture
at its worst. End Section 230!

Dec 27, 2020

$2000 + $2000 plus other family members.
Not $600. Remember, it was China's fault!

Dec 31, 2020

Twitter is shadow banning like never before.
A disgrace that our weak and
ineffective political leadership refuses
to do anything about Big Tech. They're either
afraid or stupid, nobody really knows!

Dec 31, 2020

JANUARY SIXTH, SEE YOU IN DC!

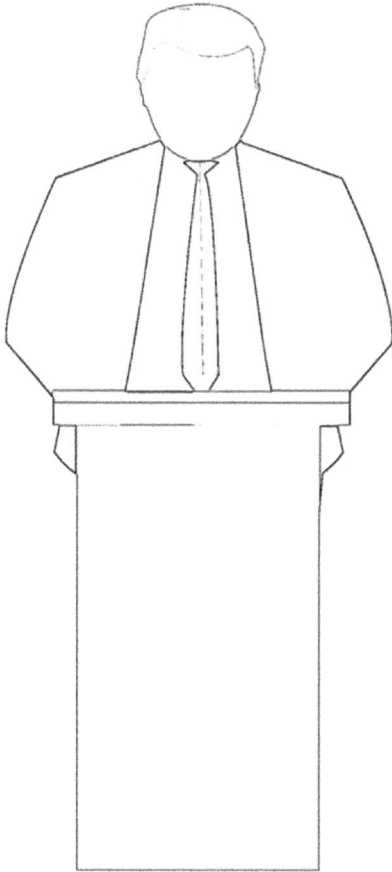

2021

MAKE AMERICA GREAT AGAIN!

Jan 4, 2021

Something how Dr. Fauci is revered
by the LameStream Media as such a great
professional, having done, they say, such an
incredible job, yet he works for me and the
Trump Administration, and I am in no
way given any credit for my work. Gee,
could this just be more Fake News?

Jan 6, 2021

The Vice President has the power to reject
fraudulently chosen electors.

Jan 6, 2021

Washington is being inundated with
people who don't want to see an
election victory stolen by emboldened Radical
Left Democrats. Our Country has had enough,
they won't take it anymore! We hear you
(and love you) from the Oval Office.
MAKE AMERICA GREAT AGAIN!

Jan 6, 2021

Antifa is a Terrorist Organization,
stay out of Washington. Law enforcement is
watching you very closely!
@DeptofDefense @TheJusticeDept
@DHSgov @DHS_Wolf @SecBernhardt
@SecretService @FBI

Jan 6, 2021

If Vice President @Mike_Pence comes
through for us, we will win the Presidency.
Many States want to decertify the
mistake they made in certifying incorrect &
even fraudulent numbers in a process
NOT approved by their State Legislatures
(which it must be). Mike can send it back!

Jan 6, 2021

Even Mexico uses Voter I.D.

Jan 6, 2021

Mike Pence didn't have the courage
to do what should have been done to
protect our Country and our Cosntitution,
giving States a chance to certify a corrected
set of facts, not the fraudulent or
inaccurate ons which they were asked to
previously certify. USA demands the truth!

*This claim of election fraud is disputed,
and this Tweet can't be replied to, Retweeted,
or liked due to a risk of violence*

Jan 6, 2021

Please support our Capitol Police and
Law Enforcement. They are truly on
the side of our Country. Stay peaceful!

Jan 6, 2021

I am asking for everyone at the U.S. Capitol
to remain peaceful. No violence!
Remember, WE are the Party of
Law & Order – respect the Law and our great
men and women in Blue. Thank you!

Jan 6, 2021

> *This Tweet is no longer available because*
> *it violated the Twitter Rules*

Jan 6, 2021

> *This Tweet is no longer available because*
> *it violated the Twitter Rules.*

Jan 6, 2021

> *This Tweet is no longer available because*
> *it violated the Twitter Rules.*

Jan 7, 2021

"As a result of the unprecedented and
ongoing violent situation in
Washington, D.C., we have required the
removal of three @realDonaldTrump
Tweets that were posted earlier today for
repeated and severe violations of our
Civic Integrity policy.

This means that the account of
@realDonaldTrump will be locked for
12 hours following the removal of these Tweets.
If the Tweets are not removed, the account
will remain locked."
— @TwitterSafety

Jan 8, 2021

The 75,000,000 great American Patriots
who voted for me, AMERICA FIRST,
and MAKE AMERICA GREAT AGAIN,
will have a GIANT VOICE long into
the future. They will not be disrespected or
treated unfairly in any way, shape or form!!!

Jan 8, 2021

To all of those who have asked,
I will not be going to the Inauguration
on January 20th.

*Twitter has permanently suspended the
@realDonaldTrump account.*

INDEX

www.ingramcontent.com/pod-product-compliance
Lightning Source LLC
Chambersburg PA
CBHW070015100426
42740CB00013B/2507

* 9 780648 823681 *